D0244878

THE
**REPAIR
SHOP**

THE REPAIR SHOP

TALES FROM THE WORKSHOP OF DREAMS

KAREN FARRINGTON

Foreword by Jay Blades

BOOKS

With special thanks to *The Repair Shop*'s experts
for their contributions to this book.

1

BBC Books, an imprint of Ebury Publishing
20 Vauxhall Bridge Road,
London SW1V 2SA

BBC Books is part of the Penguin Random House group of companies
whose addresses can be found at global.penguinrandomhouse.com

Main text by Karen Farrington

This book is published to accompany the television series entitled
The Repair Shop, first broadcast on BBC Two in 2017

First published by BBC Books in 2020
Paperback edition published in 2022

www.penguin.co.uk

A CIP catalogue record for this book is available from the British Library

ISBN 9781785947667

Printed and bound in Great Britain by Clays Ltd, Elcograf S.p.A.

The authorised representative in the EEA is Penguin Random House Ireland,
Morrison Chambers, 32 Nassau Street, Dublin D02 YH68

Penguin Random House is committed to a sustainable future
for our business, our readers and our planet. This book is made
from Forest Stewardship Council® certified paper

CONTENTS

Foreword by Jay Blades   vii

A Jamaican Pump Organ   1
A Silver-Plated Samovar   17
A Ceramic Bowl From Danzig   29
A Propeller Clock   41
Carved Wooden Angels   53
A Foundling's Teddy   65
A Bletchley Park Bicycle   77
A Captain Scott Album   91
An Airman's Jacket   105
A Lantern Clock   119
The Bedford Theatre Windows   129
A Strongwoman's Dress   143
A Fairground Water Can   157
A Butter Churn   169
A Miner's Lamp   181
A Village School's Deeds   195
A 'Rusty Bucket'   211
A Sewing Table   223
A Lifeboat Binnacle   237

FOREWORD

No matter how damaged, there is always a way to bring the things you love back to life.

Having worked on *The Repair Shop*, I've learnt everything that has a past can have a beautiful future too. We have experts who will lavish time and expertise on items that might otherwise be thrown onto the scrap heap. And some things are too precious to be discarded, not because they are worth lots of money, but for the memories they evoke of an era that's gone but not forgotten. Here in the workshop, there's never a time when objects are written off for being too difficult or time-consuming to fix.

Our experts are extraordinary. All of them are undisputed masters of their craft – but it's more than that. When objects in need of repair turn up on their work benches, it is mostly broad experience, but also a bit of intuition, that leads them to make choices about how to best bring something back to life. When there's doubt, there are plenty of other people to consult who share the same deep-rooted concern for conservation. That's a well of knowledge that will never run dry.

Watching talented hands do exquisite work never grows old with viewers, who can pick up tips and techniques for restoration projects of their own. But in addition, there are the compelling stories attached to each item, which range from romantic and sentimental to downright terrifying. Well-worn objects can be a symbol of courage or a badge of honour, a memorial to an ancestor or a reminder of a way of life that few know. Sometimes the stories chime with each of us, resurrecting a buried memory from childhood. But it might be a tale so tailored to one family it leaves us awe-inspired about what others have confronted in times more treacherous than our own. History teaches us how lessons from the past can arm us for tomorrow. All of us want to celebrate our heritage and this is an ideal way to do it.

In the show, there are plenty of moments charged with raw emotion. It's very daunting for contributors to come before cameras when they've probably never been on television before – and they often get caught by the feelings that well up inside.

Forgetting all about the cameras, we respond with a listening ear because it is beautiful to hear their stories. We don't know how they are going to react or what might trigger tears, but it's good to connect with something at their core.

At the big reveal, the experts are also nervous, hoping their nuanced approach proves the right one with the owner. I'm happy to say that they are not only almost always on target but are scoring bull's-eyes. Our craftspeople always fall a little bit in love with an item while they work on it, too. There's nostalgia, certainly, and sometimes we all end up feeling sentimental together, but whatever the responses shown on screen, they all run deep.

Everyone has a story to tell. For those who can link their family history to a symbolic object, we at *The Repair Shop* can play a role in its retelling. We feel privileged at becoming a small part of that history.

Jay Blades

A JAMAICAN
PUMP ORGAN

Vera McKenzie had her small feet planted firmly on the gently rolling deck as she gazed at the grey outline of England's south coast pressing into view. Expectant and anxious, she was one of thousands who came from the West Indies in answer to a clarion call for workers to rebuild Britain following the Second World War and she was confident of a warm welcome from a mother country in dire need. But she was worried that husband Herbert, or Mack, who had made the same journey nine months previously, would not be on the dockside to meet her. If he wasn't there, how would she carry a precious possession that had accompanied her on the voyage down the gangplank and off the docks?

When Vera left Kingston, Jamaica, aged 34, she was forced to part with almost all her possessions, being restricted to just a suitcase of clothing. But in that torment of stark choices, she found she couldn't contemplate leaving her cherished pump organ behind. The hefty instrument, also known as a reed organ or harmonium, is a cousin to the accordion and Vera's had been presented to her by a music teacher. Its sound had become a mainstay of her leisure time, which would endure at the heart of her family and religious life. Only when a well-meaning home fix ended in disaster many years later would it be silenced. Years after that, thanks to the skills of the team at the Repair Shop, it was finally brought back to life in time to mark the centenary of Vera's birth.

But now, with the ship edging its way into the Solent, Vera's heart was racing as she considered what she might do if she found herself

alone at Southampton. Bulky and heavy, the pump organ was too difficult for Vera to lift with her slight frame. Indeed, it really needed two
willing men – grappling with the handles at each end – to shift it.

Until now, her progress through life had been sure-footed. But post-
cards sent by Vera even as the voyage to Britain was underway reveal a
new tremor of uncertainty.

One dispatched as the ship toured the Caribbean picking up passengers in July 1954 revealed she thought her destination was London.
'Dear Mackie, I am still keeping well darling. Just praying that we will
land safe. Keep well till I get there and try to find out when we are reaching London.'

A week later, another was sent from Bermuda, by which time she
was not convinced of her journey's end. 'I don't know if we will go to
shore, for we didn't in Cuba, but everything is alright up to now. I wish
you could find out where we are landing in England and meet me there
instead of London. Be good darling.' It was signed simply V.

However, as the stout ship's ropes were secured at the docks her
concerns fell away when Mack's unmistakable outline became visible
in the crowd. The pump organ had survived its month-long 4,600-mile
journey unscathed.

Vera's story begins in Siloah, Jamaica, in March 1920, where she was the product of an illicit love affair. Her father was Alexander Jhagroo, the son of an indentured worker from India, who laboured on the renowned Appleton Sugar Estate. When Vera was a toddler, her mother Mary Mundy was sent away to Costa Rica to work, to escape the perceived shame of being an unmarried mother in a strongly Presbyterian household. Vera's last memory of her mother was being bathed by her in a sunny courtyard, with Mary singing 'Yes, we have no bananas'. Although later they wrote to one another regularly, the pair never met again. While her father went on to marry someone else he remained supportive of Vera as she grew up and she became close to her half-siblings.

Brought up by her mother's parents, amid the lush hillsides in south-west Jamaica, Vera had many pastimes, including music lessons. Soon her teenage fingers flew expertly over the keys of a tutor's pump organ, made compact when its legs were collapsed. Her feet pressed the foot pedals to feed bellows, which were attached to what's known as a wind chest in which the keyboard sat. When a key was pressed it opened a valve, which pulled the vacuum through the reeds, giving it a delicate and distinctive sound.

The resonance of the notes may not have been as expansive as church organs, which have towering pipes and lengthy keyboards, but the principle was the same. Portable pump organs like this one were in fact designed for long-haul travel, being used by Christian missionaries across the world. But generally, missionaries with pump organs had wheeled transport or an army of helpers at their disposal to do the hauling.

It seems Vera's teacher was so impressed with her that she had presented her talented pupil with the pump organ and a *Songs of Praise* hymn book from which to play. An inscription in the hymn book reveals the teacher was 55-year-old Dorcas E Branday. The date, 27 September 1936, presumably marks the moment Vera finished school, left home and went to the island's capital, Kingston, to find work as a trainee seamstress. She took with her both the pump organ and hymn book, containing its treasured tunes.

Helping out at an aunt's café in Kingston, Vera met her future husband, although on first catching sight of Herbert Arnold McKenzie she thought, 'well, he is very full of himself'. He was an apprentice carpenter from the St Thomas area of east Jamaica. When his father Reuben died suddenly, his mother Keturah had a breakdown, so Mack had left school as a young teenager in order to support his mother and younger brother.

Although Jamaica was part of the British Empire, the Second World War seemed a distant conflict to many of those living on the island. Nonetheless, there were plenty, including Mack, who wanted to play their part. His plans to join 6,000 West Indians in the Allied Air Forces were thwarted, however, when Vera begged him to stay closer to home, doing something less lethal. He compromised by going to Philadelphia to work in a munitions factory that fuelled the American war effort, one of 40,000 men from the Caribbean to do so. At the start of the war, discrimination against African-Americans on their home territory was palpable, with many barred from well-paid factory jobs by powerful unions. As discontent on all sides brewed, President Franklin D. Roosevelt issued an executive order in June 1941 banning discrimination in the defensive industries. Although industrial relations in America were difficult, trade union relations were also volatile in Jamaica at the time.

While Mack was away, Jamaica was devastated by a hurricane so powerful it destroyed 40 per cent of the coconut crop and was particularly damaging in the St Thomas region. In Kingston, Vera had to learn to live without a roof after it was ripped off by the vicious winds that struck in August 1944. She was one of the lucky ones, as thousands died or were made homeless. With all resources being directed to the war effort, the island received little assistance from Britain.

The end of the war brought Mack back to Jamaica, where he and Vera married on 14 January 1946. Although the economy was struggling, the couple enjoyed a good life. Thanks to his carpentry skills, they had furniture made from the best mahogany and, as a seamstress, she could dress them both in high-quality clothes.

There were two further major hurricanes in 1950 and 1951, pegging back the financial recovery to which islanders were pinning their hopes.

Herbert and Vera

Ambitious young men like Mack began to look elsewhere to provide a safer home and a more prosperous way of living. Initial thoughts of heading back to America were dispelled by a friend who was taking up the invitation issued by Britain to staff the recovery there. They were, after all, already British subjects and while nationalism was burgeoning in Jamaica, there were many, including Mack and Vera, who felt loyalty to the hub of empire – and some who were even felt to be 'more British than the English'.

The night before Mack left in 1953 to establish a base for the couple in Britain, Vera was distraught. Throughout her life, she was a woman of few words, but now she struggled to express her feelings of impending loss. Instead, she played tunes on the pump organ that would remain special to the couple for the rest of their lives. It would be a long nine months before Vera followed.

Of course, they were not the first arrivals from the West Indies. The start of this wave of migration is usually linked to the SS *Empire Windrush*, which docked in Tilbury, Essex, on 23 June 1948 with some 490 passengers on board. However, the diaspora started years before with Jamaica's Mary Seacole nursing British soldiers in the Crimean War in the 1850s. In the years that followed, many of the 10,000 men from the Caribbean who volunteered to fight in the Second World War remained in Britain, despite widespread racism. In fact, 50 passengers from the *Windrush* headed straight to the Royal Air Force or the Army, most of them joining up for a second time, while 200 more went to stay with friends. Some of the rest stayed in the redundant air-raid shelters on Clapham Common in London.

This same year the British Nationality Act had passed, a stout open-door piece of policy giving all members of the Commonwealth the right to British citizenship. There were warm words from the then Shadow Home Secretary David Maxwell Fyfe, who said: 'We are proud that we impose no colour-bar restrictions. We must maintain our great metropolitan traditions of hospitality to everyone from every part of the empire.'

Undeniably, a bankrupt Britain was struggling in the wake of the Second World War. Although it was one of the victors, there were no spoils, simply a ruined landscape to rebuild and a population that was itching to reap a premium from the victory after years of deprivation. There were chronic manpower shortages in reconstruction, transport, manufacturing and in the newly launched National Health Service.

After he arrived, Mack headed for Birmingham, which became the biggest centre for the West Indian population outside London. Although he soon found work, there were tough times ahead in the shape of arduous shift patterns coupled with poor accommodation. Men like Mack got used to shared houses and even shared beds, with day-shift workers getting up in the morning to make way for the returning night shift. Above his bed there was a hole in an outside wall, leaving him and his possessions subject to the elements.

Thankfully he secured better housing before Vera arrived and they had a room to themselves, although this proved cold comfort at the time. As Vera arrived in Birmingham from Southampton, she saw from her train window streets of terraced housing, all with their doors firmly shut. In Jamaica, she made friends and neighbours feel welcome by keeping the door ajar.

She didn't realise that the train itself made the country seem drab, as steam locomotives pumped out dense smoke that thickly coated houses, gardens and laundry along its route. In addition, coal-fired power stations were numerous and homes were heated by open fires, usually burning the cheapest fuel. It was several years before clean-air bills made their way through Parliament to ease chronic pollution problems.

As summer made way for autumn, Vera was horrified to see all the trees apparently dying, when in Jamaica the lush landscape stayed verdant all year round. Rationing had finally ended, but still British food lacked the colour and spice she'd enjoyed.

In addition to the climate and the bland cuisine, there was a fierce undercurrent of racism that spilt over into everyday life, deeply affecting those as sensitive as Vera. Signs on shop doors instructed: 'No blacks, no Irish, no dogs.' Although she had excellent skills under her belt, she was turned away from factories by people who told her frankly 'we don't hire blacks here'. She and Mack were even abused in the street. There were many occasions when Vera sat in their room and wept. But it was

Angie and Carmen on their doorstep in 1964

at times like this that the organ became her chief comfort, its consoling familiarity in shape and sound shielding her from some of the worst effects of homesickness.

As months slipped by she became more accustomed to life in the UK, getting a factory job and finding a welcome in a Baptist church. She began making friends in both the black and white communities and thoughts of returning home to Jamaica began to recede.

And beyond Birmingham, the world was changing fast as Britain shed its colonies rapidly, hoping to avoid any damaging wars of independence. Jamaica gained independence in 1962 although, as a Commonwealth country, it continued to recognise the British monarch. That same year, changes were made in British law to restrict immigration, effectively closing the door.

One disappointment remained for Vera. Her dreams of becoming a nurse were ended by Mack, who uncharacteristically stepped in to block her plans. He feared she would be destined to carry out the most menial tasks on the ward – something the first black nurses later testified was indeed the case. He himself was overlooked for promotion on several occasions, although newly installed foremen at the factory where he worked were quick to seek his advice.

When Vera became pregnant with daughter Carmen, Mack vowed to secure better housing, finally buying a semi-detached home in Grasmere Road, Handsworth. He was helped by a pardner scheme, imported to the UK by West Indians struggling to find a fair deal in a society where equal opportunity was sometimes hard to find. A pardner scheme was like a co-operative, in that it involved people putting sums of cash into a scheme that would eventually pay out a larger lump sum that reflected their contributions. While there was no interest, there were no administration fees either. When West Indians were denied loans for housing, they used pardner schemes to find the necessary deposits for purchase. As his position in the black community elevated, Mack ran schemes to help others in the same position.

Bringing up daughters Carmen and Angela were happy times. As a stay-at-home mum, Vera not only cared for her own children but for others in the street whose parents were compelled to work. Often she led a snake of youngsters to and from school as their parents couldn't, and her kitchen was frequently filled with latch-key children from around the neighbourhood.

Tunes from the pump organ became the soundtrack of a happy childhood for both girls. On Sundays they were ushered into the front room, kept 'for best', to sing hymns. 'What a friend we have in Jesus' was Vera's favourite. At other times, Mack would break into song, in a baritone voice they were convinced sounded as good, if not better, than American crooner Jim Reeves, to be joined within moments by Vera on the organ.

Even when they were young, the girls played on the pump organ with Carmen typically on her hands and knees, pressing the foot pedals, while Angela sat on the stool, hitting the notes.

Early on, Vera taught the girls scales and simple tunes from the Smallwood's tutorial book, which was widely used at the time. As they both seemed to relish playing, their parents splashed out to buy a piano for them. But for Vera, the sound of the pump organ never lost its magic.

When a couple of the notes began to sound like flat bagpipes rather than organ music, Mack attempted a repair. But wear and tear meant the bellows were now leaky and could not hold a note, and Mack's fix rendered the instrument useless. The girls now had the piano to develop their music skills, but Vera and Mack never got rid of the organ. With their daughters, they returned to Jamaica just once, meeting up with relations and revisiting former family homes. Revelling in island life, their daughters demanded to know why their parents had left the sun-soaked paradise. 'We were told we were needed,' Mack replied sombrely.

When she became a grandmother, Vera chose to care for her daughters' children so they could return to work. She and Mack had long since become pillars of the community in Handsworth and she remained a familiar figure there until her health began to falter. Suffering from Ménière's disease, which affects balance and hearing, she also suffered two small strokes before dying in 1994 from the effects of a major one. Mack died six years later after suffering from cancer. They are buried

Angie and Carmen

Herbert and Vera in later life

together under a headstone with a heartfelt message that was sent to Carmen and Angela after Mack's death by a friend and reflects the inspiring and long-lasting effect he had on his community: 'You will only die when every person you have ever known has died.'

Carmen and husband Trevor finally moved into Grasmere Road, the house where she'd grown up, and kept the broken pump organ as a memento of her mother. Sat by the stairs, its case was decorated with lines of paint when the balustrade was redecorated.

For *The Repair Shop* expert David Burville, the pump organ instantly presented something of a mystery. Instruments like these, with rubber-ised bellows creating a vacuum to pull air in through the reeds, were made predominantly in America (rival French models usually had leather bellows with foot pedals that pushed air out over the reeds). Yet there was nothing that matched its unusual design in the catalogues and refer-ence books he keeps at his workshop in Canterbury, Kent. He eventu-ally found a small British manufacturer that made collapsible organs like Vera's with a similarly shaped piece of wood that held the legs in position when it was upright. It means the instrument was probably made in the UK at around the turn of the twentieth century.

For David, a passion with instruments like these began in child-hood, instilled in him by his father – an expert in pianolas operated by perforated cards – who travelled with a large mechanical dance organ around steam fairs and shows in Britain and on the Continent. David later did apprenticeships relating to church organs in Britain and dance organs on the Continent before establishing himself as a repairer. When he is presented with instruments like these, he needs to draw on a range of skills, involving engineering, leatherwork and cabinet making, to complete the job.

To find out why the organ wasn't working, he took it apart and discovered damage to some of the keys and valves, undoubtedly caused years ago by a spilt drink. The keys are made of wood coated in celluloid, a tough compound used from the 1870s as a replacement for ivory.

It wasn't the only unexpected find either. He also discovered a bubblegum card featuring an Olympic athlete, historic post office receipts and the teaspoon from a doll's tea set, all posted inside by Carmen and Angela when they were young.

But the primary problem was creases in the bellows cloth that, thanks to great age and enthusiastic use, were now split. David resolved this by applying leather patches to worn areas, then coating everything in a rubber solution to disguise the patches and make the bellows not only airtight again but much more robust.

The webbing that allowed the foot pedals to flex, thus working the bellows, was another pivotal problem and it also had to be replaced before the pump organ would hold a tune again. With instruments like this that work by vacuum, it's not only air drawn inside but dust and fluff. The reeds consist of brass units with tongues that flap to produce the various notes, just like a mouth organ. A thorough cleaning of all of these was also needed to bring its harmony back.

With its tulipwood case re-polished and the buckled legs revamped, the rejuvenated pump organ was ready to be returned to the sisters in an emotional reunion. David devoted about six days to the repair before it was returned to the kind of pristine condition that Vera prized so highly. The organ is now kept at Angela's house, where she plays in memory of a beloved mum and a much-missed dad.

'Mum was a woman of few words,' said Angela, 'although when she talked, everybody listened. As a young woman she would always choose to play rather than speak. Now it feels like she is being heard again in our family.'

A SILVER-PLATED SAMOVAR

S ometimes age can fog the picture of family festivities drawn from the dark recesses of the past, just as old colour photographs will fade in the light. But when he closes his eyes, one boyhood memory stays sharply imprinted in 76-year-old Nawzad Khurshid's mind.

The scene is his family home in Kirkuk, northern Iraq, after supper and with night drawing in. Everyone is gathered around a tea-maker called a samovar, exchanging stories; some of the recounted tales are funny, a few rather sad.

The plush wool of the patterned Iranian carpet he sat on was warm against his bare legs. His nose twitched at the smell of the Ceylon tea brewing, the bold flavour of its long, wiry, stewed leaves sweetened with uncounted spoons of sugar. As the tea was being drunk, the symphony of the bubbling samovar sitting on a circular tray at the heart of the family group faded and was replaced with the voices of his mother, father and grandmother, relating the details of ancestors and other heroes from their community.

With seven siblings, Nawzad squatted in the courtyard of the house during the summer. In winter, the night-time ritual took place in the hall, where the heat thrown out by the samovar was a welcome antidote to the crisp night air.

Always at the core of this poignant tradition was the samovar, an early household appliance that originated in Russia. Although there are more ancient examples, the manufacture of the modern samovar generally dates from 1778, when they became a 'must have' in Russian homes.

Soon their use spread around the region, where the heated samovar became characteristic of warm hospitality. Sometimes a teapot was kept warming on its funnel while the water was being boiled, while the process almost always demanded a sieve to stop tea leaves sloshing into the cups.

Samovars come in different styles and sizes, but the one brought into the Repair Shop looked like a cauldron with a chimney and was originally a gleaming silver in colour. Both the lid and the chimney can be removed; the lid to add water to the bowl of the samovar, which is drawn from a decorative tap when it's hot, and the chimney to more easily access the inner compartment for hot coals. Coals must be lit before they are popped into the compartment and the water comes up to boiling temperature rapidly, puffing through a pressure-release valve in the lid when it is ready.

Made in Russia, the silver-plated samovar had been bought second-hand by Nawzad's mother Najiba Mustafa in 1928 to mark her marriage to his father, Rafiq. Years afterwards, she gave it to Nawzad and his wife Karen, who were married in the UK more than 50 years ago.

The memory of it epitomises a flawless childhood from the early fifties, but Iraq was destined to soon unravel in a series of conflicts that have left the country scarred and even dangerous. When it became clear that Iraq was about to be enveloped in a terrible war, Nawzad, Karen and their three sons fled, abandoning their house, car and all their other belongings. But one cherished item they could not leave behind that grim day in June 1980 was the samovar, which travelled with them to London in a plastic carrier bag. Nawzad hugged it close to his chest as their flight left Baghdad, not knowing when he looked out of the window if he would ever see his homeland again.

When Nawzad and Karen brought the samovar into the Repair Shop it had been diminished by wear and tear, and dulled by the passing of time. Nawzad wasn't concerned about removing the dent on the front. It happened, he recalled, in a house move when his mother had asked his eldest brother to carry out the samovar – and the unlucky boy had tripped, damaging it in the fall.

But Nawzad wanted to make tea again, just as his parents had, this time for his grandchildren so he could relate stories about times past,

Nawzad's mother Najiba Mustafa

sketching their shared heritage with words while the samovar hissed gently in the background. It wasn't just that the samovar is the only heirloom he can offer his grandchildren, it's the rich narrative associated with it, one that indelibly marked his childhood, that figures so highly. It was this priceless gift he wanted to pass on to future generations. 'The samovar is very important to us as it is the only link that we have with my family and it brings back a lot of wonderful memories of my childhood,' said Nawzad, who now only has one surviving sibling.

Before it was known as Iraq, the area between the Tigris and Euphrates rivers had been known as Mesopotamia, part of the Fertile Crescent – a boomerang-shaped segment of land famous for its agricultural abundance thanks to unusually rich soil and the early use of irrigation. It was home to numerous successful tribes and, as the place where writing, the wheel and urban living first evolved, it's often called the 'cradle of civilisation'.

From the sixteenth century, the region was under the control of the Ottoman Empire, which fostered tolerance among the many diverse people under its umbrella. In 1914, the Ottoman Empire chose to fight alongside Germany, inspiring a British campaign that got bogged down in mud, disease and a lack of supplies. In 1916, some 13,000 British soldiers surrendered to the Turks at Kut, after several attempts to lift

the siege there failed at enormous human cost. It was one of the biggest humiliations ever suffered by the British army. The following year, a British campaign, which came from the west via Palestine, was finally successful and got as far as occupying Baghdad.

The Ottoman Empire did not survive the First World War. It was dismembered by the victors and a country now defined as Iraq became a British Mandate, at a time when its potential oil wealth had just been flagged and the use of oil in the First World War had underlined its critical importance. A Hashemite monarch was installed under British protection. In the twenties, when the oil wealth in the region, specifically at Kirkuk, finally became apparent, the British, French and Americans united to make sure that they were the chief beneficiaries of this 'black gold' through the newly formed Iraq Petroleum Company. Although there were an estimated 16 billion barrels beneath Kirkuk, the oil business was Iraqi only in name. However, Iraq was finally granted independence on 3 October 1932 and during the Second World War, the country aligned itself with Germany and was promptly invaded by Britain.

Regardless of international politics, when Nawzad was born in 1944 Kirkuk still bore the same character it had done for centuries. He was born into a Muslim family of Turkish descent, although his next-door neighbour was Jewish and many of his family's friends were Christian. While the majority of the population there were Turkmen like himself, there were also significant populations of Arabs, Kurds, Assyrians and Armenians in this ancient settlement, which had grown up over centuries on a plain at the foot of the Zagros Mountains.

The tomb of the prophet Daniel is claimed for Kirkuk, where a synagogue was made into a church, which is now a mosque – reflecting the historical mix of faiths.

As a child, Nawzad grew up speaking Turkish but learned Arabic at school. Like all his friends, he dreamt of becoming an oilman as the industry, with all its workers, played such a major part in the town's economy.

For him, life would indeed be intricately bound up with the fortunes of the oil industry and all the international difficulties that brought with it. His academic achievements were such that he was sponsored by the

Iraqi government to take A levels in London, followed by a degree in geology at Queen Mary University. That's where he met Karen. 'She was assistant catering manager and I was a hungry student,' he recalled.

Afterwards, he did a post-graduate qualification in petroleum engineering at London's prestigious Imperial College and, to fulfil his contract with the government, he returned to Iraq with Karen and they began a family. Working in the oil industry, he spoke English and learned French, Russian and German to better conduct business.

In 1979 Saddam Hussein came to power in Iraq and was quickly the country's unopposed dictator. Festering religious and political issues with neighbouring Iran began to boil over. By now, Nawzad was working for a British concern in Basra, which lies relatively close to the Iranian border. A grave reality struck him: war was approaching and he and his family were in the front line. He might even be compelled to abandon his wife and sons to fight in the army. When Iran began shelling border posts prior to a declaration of hostilities, he and Karen, together with their children, walked out of their home and closed the door without looking back. Claiming they were taking a flight to London to see family, they headed to Baghdad, with nothing more than a few suitcases – and a samovar – so as not to arouse suspicion. Already a notoriously brutal ruler, it's unlikely Saddam would have countenanced Nawzad's permanent departure.

The Iran-Iraq war lasted for eight years and killed about one million people. Although Iran had numerical supremacy, it struggled to make definitive gains because Iraq boasted more firepower and air superiority. Tanker traffic in the Persian Gulf became a target and the international fixation on oil meant warships from countries like the US and Britain were beckoned into the fray. Another proxy war was conducted against the Kurds, who wanted a homeland, with 5,000 civilians killed in a single chemical attack launched by Iraq. Nawzad and Karen watched from afar and in dismay as the body count mounted up. But it wasn't the end of Iraq's problems.

A decade later, Nawzad was working for a petroleum company in Kuwait when Saddam Hussein's forces invaded. Luckily, he was visiting

Nawzad's wife Karen and their sons soon after leaving Iraq

London at the time, but he lost his home, his car and all his belongings for a second time. It seemed that for Nawzad, returning to his childhood home was now too perilous to consider.

However, he did visit Iraq again, for a short business trip in 2004, attending meetings at the Ministry of Oil in Baghdad. Although he had dreamt of returning to his homeland, this journey seemed hauntingly unreal, with the capital bearing little resemblance to the city he had once known. It was soon after the second Gulf War, but the shattering effects of the long insurgency were not yet apparent. American tanks were still roaming the rubble-strewn streets and at night the peace was shattered by gunfire from the Green Zone nearby. When the week-long trip was over, knowing it might have been a final visit, one part of him yearned to stay in his homeland. Yet he was also filled with joy and relief at being able to go back to his family, to live with all the unspoken guarantees that peace and security bring.

Samovars are still popular today in Russia, Iran, Iraq and other countries, but new models are heated by kerosene or even electricity and are a popular buy for tourists in the region.

To defend against its boiling heat, Nawzad's samovar had matching wooden handles on the sides and thus it could be safely moved. But the corresponding handles from its chimney and tap were missing. Using a lathe, Will turned a new wooden handle for the chimney, putting ribs where the palm would grasp it, and also made a knob for the tap. Then he colour-matched them so they seemed the same vintage as the existing handles.

For Brenton, the chief issue initially was to fix the catch on the door beneath the samovar, which was there to trap the ash when the heated charcoal burnt itself out. The door itself was intact, but the turning catch was failing. Planning a model on paper first, Brenton went on to cut out the necessary metal shape that would make the fastening and solder it in to place.

Polishing the samovar may have been the final job, but it would also be the longest. As Brenton predicted, it needed considerable amounts of elbow grease to achieve the kind of shine he was hoping for and, at first, it seemed like the polish was making little difference. He pointed out that the first pass on the bodywork of the samovar felt gritty, but after a spell of rubbing it was smooth. When he used a soft cloth on the same area, it finally came up with a shiny lustre.

When the samovar was unveiled to Nawzad and Karen, the wonder that filled their faces was reflected back at them like a mirror in the bulbous body of the container.

'It's a miracle, I didn't expect it to look this good,' Nawzad confessed. 'It takes me back many decades.'

The samovar, buffed and beautiful, was ready to resume its central position in home life. There it could connect the youngest grandchild to a distant corner of northern Iraq, where life 70 years ago was tranquil and filled with the certainty that the love of a close family brings. With Nawzad visibly moved at the sight, Jay told him: 'We are so glad to be a part of your family's history.'

A CERAMIC BOWL
FROM DANZIG

Harrowing tales of love and loss during the years of Nazi oppression have been handed down the generations, in memories more treasured than anything Hitler's supporters could have smashed or stolen.

Yet sometimes a single item becomes disproportionately precious as a token of humanity that emerged against all odds from this time of darkness.

At her workstation, ceramics expert Kirsten Ramsay surveyed seven chunky fragments of a shattered bowl that fell squarely into this category. Her task was to unite the pieces and re-create a stunning shallow dish that told parallel stories of two twentieth-century women who escaped the Holocaust.

The first was Lola Feuer, who was born in Danzig (now Gdańsk) in 1909. At the time the city was part of the German Empire led by Kaiser Wilhelm II and the First World War was five years away. When the conflict began, the front line was far away in France and Lola was just a child, but she would certainly remember the hunger that Germans suffered during a British naval blockade.

When Germany surrendered at the end of the war, the entire nation was subjected to a harsh peace settlement rather than a just one. With the Treaty of Versailles, Danzig became a free city administered by the League of Nations, a newly sculpted international body in which a generation scarred by the horrors of large-scale hostilities invested their hopes for on-going world peace.

A pinprick on the globe, Danzig became an international 'special case' for its strategic position as a port on the Baltic Sea – and ended up in the eye of a fearful storm. Geographically, its neighbours were now Poland – historically a country in its own right but frequently occupied by neighbouring superpowers – and East Prussia, which was part of, but isolated from, a much-reduced Germany. The so-called Polish corridor, which was designed to give Poland access to the sea, split the body of Germany from East Prussia and butted up against Danzig, becoming a festering sore for the recently defeated nation, now stripped of its territorial assets and burdened by the immense debt of bearing the costs of war.

Although the majority of Danzig's residents were, like Lola, of German heritage, it was Poland who controlled tariffs, customs and vital access points. And while her mother tongue was German, she and thousands of others who had so recently called the Kaiser their emperor were stripped of German citizenship. Lola was one of an estimated 3,000 Jews – both German and Polish – in the city and its immediate surroundings.

On one side Poland tried to assert more authority in the region, building for itself a new port to rival Danzig. On the other, there was muscle-flexing from Germany as it became driven by a new-found virulent nationalism that culminated in Hitler's fascist rule.

Although living at the heart of a complex political dynamic, life continued in relative normality for Lola. She went to college, then worked in a medical science laboratory. And she met and married Hermann, who came from Tarnów, which at the time of his birth was part of the teetering Habsburg Empire. Despite long, drawn-out internal squabbles, the empire, with Austria's Franz Joseph I at its head, had been the largest political realm in Europe at the outbreak of the First World War. As a young man, Hermann served in its army on horseback.

After the war, he moved first to Prague then to Danzig, where he became a director in a telecommunications company. At the time only thriving businesses could afford such luxury, but it was a booming sector nonetheless. Hermann became reasonably affluent and was well connected in the city thanks to the success of his company, numbering ethnic Germans and Poles among his close contacts.

Lola with her son Martin as a baby

As Jews, both Hermann and Lola must have watched with considerable anxiety at the events unfolding in Germany, where the Jewish population became a defenceless target of national aggression. In Danzig, nationalist fervour was being relentlessly stirred by Hitler, who pushed the agenda of German victimhood within its frontiers.

With extraordinary foresight, Hermann applied for visas to Palestine, another region that was changed by the end of the First World War. It had been part of the Ottoman Empire, another fading star of nineteenth-century geo-politics. Now Palestine was in the hands of the British, who were laying the foundations for a Jewish homeland.

Soon, offences against the Jews in Germany began to be dramatically ramped up. In November 1938, police stood idly by as paramilitaries allied with ordinary people went on the rampage in Germany, wrecking Jewish shops, businesses and synagogues. It was an extraordinary departure from civilised behaviour. The death toll that night is unknown, but some 30,000 men were torn away from their families and incarcerated in concentration camps. For anyone who'd managed to ignore the growing momentum of dangerous anti-Semitism, the cruel intentions of the Nazi

regime were now writ large. Just one month later, Hermann received a stark warning from a contact: leave now as your arrest is imminent.

Immediately, he set off for Tarnów to warn his family of the looming threat. The Treaty of Versailles had placed the town in Polish jurisdiction and although his father had died, Hermann's mother, sister and brother still lived there with his young niece, Nora. Alas, his relatives were deaf to his worried words, convinced their future was irrevocably tied to their past. Hermann wanted to take Nora to Palestine and care for her there as he would a daughter, but on the morning of his departure, his family hid the girl so she remained in Tarnów.

Meanwhile, Lola was left to pack up their Danzig home so their belongings could be shipped to Palestine, whilst looking after toddler Martin. Much of the population was by now infected with anti-Semitism and the removal men, numbed by years of Nazi propaganda, were no exception. Lola could only stand by in silence as they randomly smashed the couple's belongings, laughing as they did so, while shielding three-year-old Martin from the worst effects of the intimidation. Only when they arrived in Palestine on 28 December 1938 could Lola and Hermann finally breathe a sigh of relief. They made a home in Tel Aviv, where a decorated dish that remarkably had survived the trip from Danzig took its place on the dresser. It wasn't all plain sailing, but they fared far better than Hermann's family who opted to stay in Tarnów.

After the Germans invaded Poland at the start of September 1939, measures against the town's 25,000 Jewish population began. After special taxes, fines and forced labour came deportations and killings. Hundreds were taken from a ghetto created in the town to be massacred in the cemetery. None of Hermann's family survived.

As for the Feuers, Martin celebrated his Barmitzvah on the same day the British flag was lowered in Palestine and the nation of Israel was forged. After a spell in the Israeli army, he came to England to study at Battersea College, then married Angela. They lived in northwest London while he worked in hotel management.

Ultimately, Martin was reunited with the Danzig bowl that had been a small but constant part of his ruptured childhood, eventually giving it

Martin aged 4 or 5, with the bowl
on the dresser behind him

to his daughter Penny. After Lola's death in 1999, it represented both a celebration of survival and victory over tyranny. Penny's emotional feelings about the bowl and the ties to her family were further impacted when Martin died in 2015.

But a mistimed jump by Penny's ragdoll cat Mittens left the cherished ceramic in pieces and Penny forlorn. For her, the dish was a precious tangible link to her grandmother's story. At the time, she didn't know the bowl also represented another woman's triumph over Nazi oppression. In fact, its elegant shape and vintage glazes were characteristic of creator Grete Marks, another German Jew who likewise escaped the worst of Nazi terror, although not without personal cost.

* * *

Also known as Margarete Heymann or Heyman-Lobenstein, Grete Marks was born in Cologne and initially studied art in the city before moving to the Academy of Fine Arts in Dusseldorf.

In 1920 she applied to the Bauhaus, the iconic German art school that became famous for its exploration of form and function, becoming one of its few women pupils. Swiss artist Paul Klee and Russian Wassily Kandinsky were lecturers while she was there.

Grete started with a preliminary course and a trial term in the ceramics class, but her efforts to progress were dogged by stout opposition from tutors. On 21 June 1921, the records declare: 'Miss Heymann will only receive final notification of the end of the semester as her suitability for craft work (pottery) cannot yet in principle be assessed.'

In a later report, she was deemed 'probably talented' but 'not suitable' for the workshop and she was told the decision about her admission was being postponed. There are no known examples of her work from the era.

Abruptly, Grete left the Bauhaus and began to run a ceramics course for children back in Cologne. No one knows quite why, as Grete certainly embraced the modernism that was the hallmark of the Bauhaus movement, but it's thought that some of the (male) tutors believed women more suited to weaving courses.

In 1922 she worked in a stonework factory as a painter and a year later she married economist Gustav Loebenstein.

Together they rented a disused kiln and factory in Marwitz and established the Haël Workshops, through which Grete had a free hand with design. Her bold plates and tea sets were popular in a free-thinking country prior to Nazi domination. It's probably here that she made the bowl that found its way into the Repair Shop, using flourishes of cobalt blue, emerald green and cadmium yellow.

A series of catastrophes then knocked her life off its tracks. In 1928 her husband and her brother-in-law Daniel, who also worked in the business, were killed in a car accident on their way to a trade fair in Leipzig. Grete was now a single mother of two children and the sole proprietor of a successful business with 120 employees and enthusiastic markets in London and New York. But the ripple effect of the Wall Street Crash soon left customers without ready cash. Five years after she was widowed, her young son died in a fatal accident. Also in 1933, she began to feel the insidious pinch of political diktats designed to squeeze Jews out of public life. Ultimately she sold an underpriced business, which was promptly resurrected by a German designer.

Highly individual in her approach to art and life, Grete – not only Jewish but a woman who dressed in men's clothes – was a prime target in Nazi Germany. Her audacious, geometric designs were labelled 'degenerate' by the regime.

Grete spent a short spell spent in Jerusalem, trying and failing to replicate the business there. In 1936 she emigrated to the United Kingdom with the help of Ambrose Heal, the owner of a department store who'd previously bought her work. Grete began teaching at the Burslem School of Art in Stoke-on-Trent, the home of British pottery. She married for a second time to educator Harold Marks and produced ceramics commercially again, although never registering the same success that she knew in Germany. In later life, she took up painting.

* * *

In the Repair Shop barn Kirsten was contemplating the task ahead. Her brief from Penny was simple enough. 'If the bowl can be in one piece rather than seven that would just be gorgeous.'

But Kirsten quickly identified that the catastrophic breakage by the cat wasn't the first time the bowl had come to grief. Having established all the pieces of the bowl were on the bench in front of her, she decided to undo the old repair to eliminate the tell-tale line tracking along the bowl's surface.

It meant applying a generous amount of paint stripper to soften the adhesive that had been used previously, then leaving the pieces wrapped in tin foil to allow the chemicals to do their work. The aim was to gently take apart the pieces once that process was complete. However, on this occasion new methods were trumped by an old one. Whatever glue had been used on the initial repair stubbornly refused to give way. Kirsten abandoned plans to part the pieces, for to do so would risk causing further damage to the bowl. Instead, she vowed to improve the pre-existing work.

Inevitably, age had left its calling card on the glaze in the centre of the bowl and Kirsten wielded her steam cleaner to lift the ingrained dirt.

Having thoroughly cleaned the bowl and its broken edges, it was time to start the process of reassembly. As the bowl was earthenware, the break edges were consolidated to seal them before applying the adhesive. After putting dots of an adhesive along the exposed sides of one piece of shard, she offered up another, waiting for the moment of 'bite' between the two pieces when experienced hands can detect that an accurate connection has been made. Once glued, she held the pieces in place using short sections of clear tape pulled taut to recreate the natural tension lost in the piece when the breakage happened. Two hands weren't enough to work at the speed necessary for the repair, so Kirsten called Jay in to help.

With the bowl in one piece, it was time to fill in the cracks with an acrylic filler, leaving white smears in the wake of the steel spatula. Kirsten was unruffled by its scruffy appearance. With her extensive experience, she knew it would look worse before it looked better. When it was dry, the filler was sanded back with fine glass paper until the surface was smooth, then it was time for the finishing touches. Kirsten is so expert at mixing paint colours and applying them with narrow brushes that it was difficult to tell the original brushwork in the design from the barely dry. Afterwards, the earthy pigments once again appeared perfect, as it was when Grete completed it decades earlier. The restored surface was then polished to blend in with the original glaze.

Penny was overwhelmed when she saw the dish in pristine condition. 'It is more than I could have hoped for,' she admitted.

While she held her grandmother's story close to her heart, she didn't know that Grete had made the dish until after her segment was broadcast on *The Repair Shop*. When it aired, she received an email from a ceramics collector who identified the work from the screen and shared details about Grete with Penny.

Both Grete and Lola died in their nineties, reaching old age having escaped the terrible fate of so many of their countrymen and women. Despite their mirrored lives, there's no reason to believe they ever met. Penny doesn't know when her grandmother got the bowl designed by Grete, but Hermann and Lola were married in 1929, at a time when Grete's pottery was immensely popular. It's tempting to imagine it was given to them as a gift to mark the occasion. When she realised their shared experiences – and that by a quirk of fate the duo avoided the horror of the death camps – Penny felt a greater affinity to the bowl than ever before.

A PROPELLER CLOCK

Infested with lice, the target of snipers and deafened by the artillery shells whistling overhead, British soldiers in the First World War reluctantly learnt to endure the grisly realities of industrial warfare.

A gruelling marathon, First World War trench combat moved men to madness as well as poetry, and took them through all the emotional gears in between. The Western Front, which stretched from the North Sea to the Swiss frontier, wasn't perpetually ablaze nor were men constantly in the line of fire. But inside frontline trenches there were rats, raw sewage and glutinous mud. Ahead lay no-man's land, with barbed wire supporting the shattered corpses of soldiers who'd perished in failed operations. Even far behind the lines, living quarters were rudimentary and the earth still shook from artillery barrages.

When soldiers were crouching among the sandbags, pinned down by volleys of explosives and enveloped in clouds of cordite smoke or even mustard gas, their envious, stinging eyes must have sought out the tinny buzz of bi-planes overhead as they crossed the front line with apparent ease.

No surprise then that numerous Tommies dreamed of leaving their grim existence behind to blaze a trail in the Royal Flying Corps instead. Among them was Ernest Ridgway, the son of a coal merchant based in Hinckley, Leicestershire, and known to his family as Dick. Before the outbreak of war he worked as a dyer's clerk but was one of the first volunteers to sign up for his county's regiment.

Dick's army records are missing, but it's known he went to France at the beginning of March 1915 at a time when the British and French armies were shaping up for the Battle of Neuve Chapelle. Costly in terms of casualties, the campaign gained little territory and was carried out when supplies of shells were critically short. As fighting men struggled to carry out their orders against determined defenders, supporting artillery attacks were rationed for fear of running out of ammunition. For men like Dick, it must have been difficult to maintain morale or resist the temptation to seek another way of serving King and country.

He wasn't alone. Arthur Harris, a significant figure later in Britain's aerial bombardments of the Second World War, had made a similar decision. However, when he applied to join the Royal Flying Corps he was told there were 6,000 men ahead of him in the queue. Recruitment was a fast-paced operation, though.

With Germany employing deadly new aircraft weaponry, the casualty list in the Royal Air Corps was mounting and both Dick and Arthur Harris were found a place in its ranks.

Today, Dick's family can only imagine the terror of his experiences in the trenches. Yet those fearful times were followed by a different set of terrors after he joined the No. 4 Officer Cadet Battalion of the RFC in July 1916 as a second lieutenant. Now his fate was to use flimsy aircraft against well-armed opposition.

At that time, the men of the RFC dubbed it 'a suicide club' in a display of gallows humour. Even during training, would-be pilots were suffering a 50 per cent casualty rate, with men permitted to fly solo after barely an hour's tuition under their belts. According to the RAF Museum, flying instructors nicknamed their students 'Huns' because they thought that they were equally as dangerous as the enemy.

Thankfully, Dick survived training and some flights at least after joining 54 Squadron. But one mission in November that year ended in near disaster, with him being pulled from his aircraft after he crash-landed as a result of becoming an airborne target. With Dick in the safe hands of medics, the ground crew cannibalised the propeller of the plane he was in, with one of the engineers making it into a clock, more a badge of honour than a trusty timepiece. That's how Dick became

Ernest Ridgway in his Royal Flying Corps uniform

one of relatively few men to return from Flanders with something more tactile and practical than a set of medals.

From writing engraved on the propeller, it first seemed that Dick was flying a French-built Morane-Saulnier plane, which would either have been a parasol-winged scout plane, with a two-bladed propeller that became one of the first to be fitted with a machine gun, or an earlier version, remembered afterwards for its hefty handling.

However, further research revealed that the engines were used in newly launched Sopwith Pups, at the time the most superior aircraft in the field and favoured by pilots for being lighter and less dangerous than predecessors. Still, the 80hp engine that powered it was about the same size as an outboard motor today.

The clock was always prominent in the Ridgway household, with its loud tick resonating. At one stage the clockwork mechanism was replaced by an electric one. When it stopped working, the family took no less pride in it. But when they had the chance, Dick's son Tony and grandson Tom brought it into the Repair Shop for scrutiny by Steve Fletcher, hoping it could be brought back to life again.

The warm hues of the wooden propeller the timepiece is made from and its aerodynamic lines are immediately reminiscent of the early history of military flight.

Britain's Royal Flying Corps had been in existence since 1912, less than a decade after the Wright brothers had made the first controlled, powered, heavier-than-air manned flight in North Carolina. The RFC consisted of Military and Naval Wings and a Central Flying School and experimented with kites, balloons and gliders as well as aircraft as at the time it wasn't clear which form of flight would have the edge. Two years later, pilots were catapulted into a conflict that was to conclusively prove the strategic advantages of military flights.

At the start of the war, the perception was of airmen who were gung-ho aristocrats, taking to the skies with insubstantial machines and using pistols to defend themselves when they encountered enemy aircraft. With shots almost always awry, the opponents would give each other a friendly wave before heading back to land on their respective sides of the Front.

If this existed at all outside the public's imagination, it was a short-lived phase, although there certainly was a spell at the start of the conflict when the biggest threat to the health of the pilot was defects in the plane.

Initially, the RFC was tasked with aerial reconnaissance. That meant flying high across enemy territory with a photographer in position to capture evidence of newly-made trenches and troop, train or artillery movements.

However, no one was very keen to offer up their battle plans in this way to the opposing side and technology went on the march. In July 1915, German pilots got behind the joystick of the Fokker Eindecker, equipped with a gear that made it possible for them to fire a machine gun that was synchronised through spinning propellers. The period that followed was known as the 'Fokker Scourge', with German planes enjoying dominance in the skies above Flanders. British and Commonwealth pilots on the Western Front now experienced an average survival rate of 11 days. It was a year before the British were armed with planes that offered similar firepower. The first planes to be fitted with the Constantinesco synchronization, or CC gear, to enable this were the DH.4s, which went into action in March 1917, after which airborne fortunes see-sawed for a while.

By now, the pilot brief had expanded from reconnaissance to strafing troops, shooting down observation balloons and targeting roads, marshalling yards and railway stations. Bomb aiming remained nothing short of random, a technological issue that wouldn't be sorted until the Second World War was underway.

Pilots like Dick flew two missions a day, always with the risk of being shot down in flames either by German aircraft during a dog fight or machine-gun fire from the ground. It was almost relentlessly cold in the cockpit and in the winter months, tears could freeze on your face. As well as enemy aircraft, British pilots might well have been dwarfed in the sky by Zeppelin airships, with the newest class in 1916 being a colossal 198 metres in length and armed with ten machine guns. Zeppelins were both a terrifying spectacle and a vast target, used to cover greater distances and so tasked with bombing Britain. During Dick's short spell in the RFC, there were also some major airborne operations alongside daily outward expeditions.

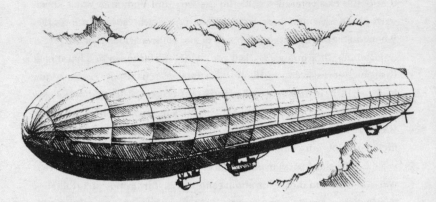

July 1916 saw the start of the Battle of the Somme, with casualties among British ground troops running to more than 57,000, including 19,000 dead, on the first day alone. RFC squadrons were also involved, along with French planes, and helped to steer that costly – and ultimately futile – push into German-held territory. The same month there were attacks by the Royal Naval Air Service on German petrol-storage facilities and the launch of a Middle East Brigade, putting RFC units in Macedonia, Mesopotamia, Palestine and East Africa under a single command. In September, a Zeppelin was shot down over Hertfordshire, ending forays by German Army airships over Britain, although those operated by the Kaiser's navy continued to penetrate the home front. Two weeks later, RFC aircraft flew in support as Britain's first tank saw action on the Western Front. The same day, and for the first time, a submarine belonging to the French was sunk by an Austrian aircraft.

Records show Dick was declared 'unfit' for duty for the first time on 3 November 1916. Afterwards, it seems he was linked to instruction rather than airborne action, a vital role for the expanding service.

Even when new technology enhanced the lot of British pilots, there were still hazards that demanded circus-style antics from airmen.

For example, in 1917 the British unveiled the S.E.5 – fast, nimble and armed with Lewis and Vickers guns. It wasn't always reliable, though, as one veteran recalled to the Imperial War Museum. 'Those guns could jam and very often did jam and when they jammed in the middle of a fight the pilot was in a very precarious position. The unjamming of a gun when you are flying at 100 miles per hour plus with icy hands at 15,000 feet was a very difficult thing because you had to put your hand out round the windscreen ... into the wind and get hold of a handle on the gun and try and jerk it over, in order to clear the belt which was a collapsible belt which used to get jammed in the breach ...'

However, the airmen returned each night to a hot meal, a warm bed and access to a mess in which to discuss the triumphs and tragedies of the preceding day with colleagues. This was a luxury unknown to the nation's foot soldiers.

In the spring of 1918, the RFC and the RNAS made way for the Royal Air Force, which inherited over 100 training squadrons and 30 specialist schools, with the number of aircraft rising exponentially.

Before the Armistice that year, would-be pilots were on the receiving end of an 11-month training course, which included 50 hours of solo flight. Inevitably, the number of air casualties tumbled.

Although Dick became part of the RAF, he was by now back in Britain at a training base in Market Drayton following his accident. By February 1918, he starting dating wife-to-be Kathleen. In a letter, in which he addresses her as Miss Beattie, he hopes that she is 'none the worse' for the late night that followed their outing. 'I must say, I enjoyed myself immensely and trust you did also.' His instincts were correct as they married in 1920, with newspaper reports revealing the bride wore a dress of cream duchess satin with an overdress of georgette and a veil wreathed in orange blossom. She had a bouquet of white carnations, roses and lilies, and bridesmaids dressed in midnight blue. The couple spent their honeymoon in London. Shortly before the Second World War, Dick returned to service in the Leicestershire Regiment, heading a platoon in a newly formed National Defence Company, formed by Secretary of State for War Leslie Hore-Belisha in February 1939 to guard vulnerable locations.

Kathleen on her wedding day in 1920

The family Dick and Kathleen had now cherishes the propeller clock as a mark of life's fragility. If Dick hadn't survived the accident, then none of them would be here today.

Steve's first task was clear. He was going to remove the outdated electrical mechanism, which he quickly diagnosed as a hazard in terms of electric shocks and fires.

After that, he removed the dial cover and the hands to discover the clock face was plastic. A crack that ran down its centre had gathered grime over the years, but dipping it in a detergent risked removing the black numerals around the edge, or parts of them.

Steve took advice from ceramics specialist Kirsten, who is an expert at cleaning up delicate surfaces. Her first suggestion was acetone, but a cotton-wool pad soaked in it came away clean after being rubbed gently across the offending crack.

The next step up in terms of strength was bleach. Kirsten applied some to a patch on the back of the clock face – with great results. This time the cotton wool was loaded with black dirt after an initial rub and the surface below was sparkling. But would the fluid erase the dial numbers? As Kirsten pointed out, it was hard to control a bleach clean.

Conservation versus restoration is a perpetual dilemma at the Repair Shop. There's a natural tension between conserving an item for future generations and restoring it, making it look like new, or at least, newer.

Gripped with a natural anxiety about putting the original numbers at risk, Steve decided against further work on the clock face. A gentle polish would have to do, with the brown fracture remaining visible.

Meanwhile, Will was reviving the natural shine of the mahogany propeller using his own concoction of cleaners to lift off generations of dirt. His plan was to apply shellac, a resin secreted by a tropical bug in the bark of trees in India and Thailand, mixed with methylated spirits to achieve a fine French polish. But all his efforts to apply the glossy finish would come to nothing if the surface wasn't properly clean. The cleaning process also helped to highlight the words and numbers etched into the propeller relating to Dick's downed plane.

Along the top are the words: 80HP LE RHONE MORANE SAULNIER, which refers to the engine to which the propeller was fitted. Inscribed around the clock face on the front is LP840 80HP LE RHONE MORANE SAULNIER D2500 P2000. The codes refer to drawing measurements in millimetres, including the pitch of the propeller.

Will now turned his attentions to a chip on the base, which he filled and then layered with polish coloured by an appropriate pigment to camouflage the patch.

Will's final task was to firmly fix the metal legs, which attached the clock to the base. The struts reflect those on the original plane with its parasol wing. To keep them firmly in place, he used hoof glue – made from horses' hooves – which is widely used in the restoration of antique furniture.

With the casing now back at Steve's work station, it was his job to fit the new battery-operated quartz movement, which would send a regular electric pulse to stimulate the clock's tick. Happily, it slotted into the existing case without difficulty. However, Steve had to enlarge the hole at the top of the clock hands, properly called a collet, to ensure a friction-tight fixing. He took a minutely cautious approach. Using a tool to shave out the heart of the collet wasn't difficult. The key to success was not to overdo it and create a hole that was simply too big.

Despite nervous moments like these, it was a joy to work on for Steve.

Tom didn't meet his grandfather. Dick died in 1951 when Tony himself was only a teenager. But he has been an unshakeable link to a conflict that's now consigned to the history books, with the clock a daily reminder of his incredible fortitude in difficult times. Back in Tom's family home, the clock is being kept for future generations so they too can glimpse the past.

CARVED
WOODEN
ANGELS

In small communities, standing proud like islands in a sea of green fields, it's not just the seasons that pace out passing time. With christenings, confirmations, marriages and funerals, churches mark the gentle rhythm of rural life for congregations, who welcome the poetry of the scriptures as much as they do fair weather and a bountiful harvest.

St Gilbert and St Hugh in Gosberton Clough is one such church, serving a ribbon-shaped hamlet on the edge of the fen. It was a latecomer to the district, which lies just outside Spalding in Lincolnshire, only making an appearance in 1902 – and even beyond that, it's a bit of an anomaly. The church was made of wood and concrete in an era when brick and stone seemed more suited to significant community buildings. Moreover, it was the work of Sir John Ninian Comper, perhaps the greatest ecclesiastical architect of the twentieth century and one of the last, with partner William Bucknall. At St Gilbert and St Hugh, Ninian Comper cast aside the weighty flourishes of the Gothic Revival for which he was best known. The design he settled on was appealingly simple yet spacious and light.

For much of its existence, unfolding events at the church have been watched over by four angels – not the celestial kind, but beautifully hand-carved wooden models made by refugees rejoicing in a safe haven. The one-of-a-kind candleholders were presented to the church during the First World War and have been witness to the village's happiest moments – including the Armistice that ended the terrible bloodshed – and its most sombre – such as the service that took place the day the Second World War was declared.

The church under construction in 1902

With time having taken its toll on the angels, here was an unusual opportunity for *The Repair Shop*'s restorer Will Kirk to save century-old religious icons, not least as a tribute to those innocent civilians who had been embroiled in the misery of conflict.

The plight of careworn Belgians who spilled over the English Channel into Britain during the opening salvoes of the war is rarely recounted. Like a history drawn in the sand, their sufferings were quickly erased by an incoming tide of chaos and carnage.

On Tuesday, 4 August 1914, German soldiers surged across the border into neutral Belgium and the First World War erupted. The Kaiser had already declared war against Russia and France and hoped for a swift victory in the west to pursue a more challenging battle in the east. He aimed to take a short cut through Belgium so that the German campaign would get off to a flying start.

Belgium's King Albert bravely rejected the German ultimatum – which violated his country's long-standing neutrality – so he and his people were reluctantly drawn into war. Given its small standing army, the diminutive but populous country could do little to thwart the incoming Germans. In turn, a treaty signed in 1839 by diplomats who had long since turned to dust propelled Britain into the conflict, having pledged to defend Belgium all those years ago. However, it would take some days to bring the British army into the fray.

Almost overnight, a vast number of Belgium's people became refugees, fleeing an advancing front line that was squeezing them towards the coast. In tandem, there was what's known as 'the rape of Belgium', a series of atrocities by the German army against Belgian citizens. An estimated 5,500 people were executed for perceived crimes perpetrated against German soldiers in a series of conquest rituals designed to terrorise the population. In retrospect, it seems likely the invaders were overwhelmed by paranoia and interpreted passive resistance both in factories and on farms as something sinister and dangerous that warranted instant, terrible reprisals.

With both sides secure in the conviction that they had God on their side, the barbarities became a political football as each tried to clamber to the moral high ground. Britain coined the phrase 'brave little Belgium' in an attempt to lure other neutral countries into its bunker, particularly America.

At the start, people retreated to Antwerp before it finally fell on 6 October. Poet Rupert Brooke, who would die from an infected mosquito bite six months later, likened the blazing city to Dante's Inferno, but then saw 'a truer Hell. Hundreds of thousands of refugees, their goods on barrows and handcarts and perambulators and wagons, moving with infinite slowness out into the night.'

To the north, the Dutch were neutral but co-operating with the Germans, while to the southwest, France was the object of German aggression. Luxembourg was invaded on the same day as Belgium. Accordingly, some 250,000 cast their eyes across the Channel, hoping for sanctuary.

The first British people to know about the rapidly evolving humanitarian disaster were living in Folkestone on the south coast. For them, France was a thin grey line on the horizon from where they half expected to see an advancing invasion flotilla.

Instead, it was boatloads of Belgian refugees that tied up at the town's harbour. A book written in 1920 about Folkestone's recent history described events:

> The earliest arrivals came in fishing craft and coal carriers. The visitors were terror-stricken and many of them absolutely refused to leave the boats. The news of the coming of the Belgians was not made public until eight or nine days later, when it appeared in the Press.

And when the refugees finally attracted the attention of the national media, *The Times* reported:

> A huge crowd gathers daily outside the closed gates of the Harbour Station and stands there for hours to watch the thousands of people landed every afternoon who pass out to take up their temporary abode here. But it is not the usual holiday crowd which Folkestone

knows so well. These sad-faced people, who walk soberly about or gather in little groups and discuss solemnly topics which are evidently of intense interest to them, are not happy rollicking, holiday-makers, nor is their language ours. There is far more French than English heard on the Leas in these days, for Folkestone is becoming a town of refugees.

Their anxious, unhappy faces were the first glimpses the British population had into the horror that this war would bring. By 5 September, the number of refugees that had filtered in through Folkestone was estimated at 18,000 – but that wasn't the end of it. On one day alone that autumn, some 60,000 people disembarked and altogether it remains the largest influx of people into Britain at any one time.

In response, the British government formed a War Refugee Committee that marshalled the men, women and children to points across Britain. While some 15,000 stayed in Folkestone, thousands more were dispatched by train into London, where reception centres had been set up at Earl's Court and Alexandra Palace. Officials were keen to hear from any community who could accommodate refugees.

When it came to a national crisis, Spalding wanted to do its bit and joined with the 2,500-strong committee structure established nationwide to provide homes and support. As it happened, the town's Catholic mission had long-established links with Belgium. Indeed, the priest Father Clement Tyck was himself Belgian and keen to help, although all churches united in offering hospitality. Spalding's committee gave a home to some of the 164 who found a welcome in the windswept rural region. Despite heroic levels of administration, no one knows just who came to Spalding nor how long they stayed but work was readily available.

Given the absence of so many working men now serving in the British army, Belgians helped to 'keep the home fires burning'. In 1914, news of the death of Rev. Edgar Torr Hudson, aged 51, the vicar of Gosberton for a decade who had been responsible for raising the money to build St Gilbert and St Hugh, reached the small community and Belgian carvers were commissioned to make a memorial. The angels, made to a design drawn up by Ninian Comper, were presented to the church the following year.

While no one knows whose hands sawed lengths of wood or dexterously turned the chisel to make four individual figures with feathered wings – or what they'd been through before they arrived in Lincolnshire – the angels became closely associated not only with Rev. Hudson but also the refugee Belgians.

It's not the only example of their handiwork in the neighbourhood. A screen in St Peter and St Paul's in Gosberton and a pulpit at St Mary's in Pinchbeck are thought to be have been carved by them also.

After the war, very few of the refugees remained in Britain as the cordial welcome had quickly worn thin. As early as January 1915, the *Exeter and Plymouth Gazette* was reflecting a growing backlash against Belgians among those who were disappointed the war had not finished at Christmas, as predicted. 'We are rendering assistance to a great number of young Belgian lads who are shirkers and who ought to be properly in the fighting line instead of walking about streets of London with their hands in their pockets.'

Disagreements erupted in Spalding between hosts and guests after the Belgians were compelled to hand over half of their wages to finance a welfare fund.

In 1918, Belgians everywhere discovered their paid employment had come to an abrupt end as hostilities ceased, with the British government mostly concerned with the country's parlous economic situation. But thanks to the carved angels, the Belgians who'd been in Spalding were quickly gone but not forgotten.

As it happened, Ninian Comper had provided the perfect platforms for the gifts. Through his work, Ninian Comper brought back what's known as the 'English Altar', something common in the late Middle Ages and also found across Medieval Europe. Its hallmark four riddel posts at the corners often supported curtains and Ninian Comper's English altars typically had angels on top of the riddel posts, but it seems he had not included them at Gosberton Clough. As such, the Belgian carvers were rectifying an omission.

Reverend Edgar Torr Hudson

Scottish-born Ninian Comper went on to far grander projects than this in a career that spanned decades as he worked until his death in 1960. He not only designed churches but also church furnishings and stained-glass windows, each of which he marked with a strawberry in memory of his father, a Scottish Episcopal priest in the slums of Aberdeen, who died suddenly and only moments after buying some of the fruit for poor children he passed in a park. Windows on the north wall of the nave at Westminster Abbey are Ninian Comper's work, along with the chapel at Downside Abbey. One of the most celebrated examples is St Mary's Church in Wellingborough, which is richly ornate, in the manner of a medieval masterpiece, although it was only completed in 1935.

His friend John Betjeman insisted that no English architect was 'better known in cathedral close and distant rectory'.

Eventually, the Gosberton angels were moved – or possibly toppled – from their lofty perches. At one stage in the early sixties, they were all coated with gloss paint. It was surely a well-intentioned effort to preserve them but the effect was clumsy. Time continued to take its toll, with one angel suffering a singed nose after a close encounter with a candle, and another losing her hands.

As Will weighed one of the angels in the palm of his hand, he paid tribute to the unknown carvers. 'That they are still in one piece is testament to the craftsmanship,' he observed.

Looking more closely at one of the angels, a glint of gold caught his eye. Paint was worn away on the cuff of an angel's robe, revealing the shimmer of gold leaf beneath.

Almost instantly, he decided that revealing this long-lost lustre would be a better choice than refurbishing the more recent paintwork. But would all the figures have sufficient quantities of gold coating after more than 100 years to make his plan a success?

Using a swab of cotton wool soaked in acetone, he rubbed gently at each face, then at all the sets of clasped hands. The test areas revealed that there was indeed a generous layer applied by the original carvers still existing beneath the gloss. Once that was established, he settled in for the lengthy task of paint removal with acetone, something that looks and smells like nail polish remover.

The end result was stunning. Now it was time to turn to running repairs, with Will himself the carver this time. After selecting a block of limewood, he began mapping out the replacement hands, using callipers to accurately measure the hands of an angel serving as a model. Although he was drawing in two dimensions, his thought processes were in 3-D when he began chipping gently away with an assortment of chisels, careful not to remove too many layers in one go. When they were completed, the hands were glued into place.

Still, it wasn't time to add gold leaf immediately. Flecks of dark red exposed in the ageing gold leaf gave the angels a mellow, vintage appearance. No good then for one angel to have bright, shiny hands that didn't match its body.

To help them blend in, Will got some Gesso – like a white acrylic paint only thinner – and mixed it with red pigment and glue to cover the new wood. The rich red result would add a vibrancy to the gold leaf when it was completed.

Gold leaf is a fine art that's existed for centuries, commonly found in Ancient Egypt, then commandeered by Christians to illustrate the light of God in the faith's iconography. Although Will enjoys applying gold leaf, the process isn't straightforward. First, it's a case of applying a thin layer of adhesive suitable for sticking thin metals. So far, so straightforward. But then it's all a matter of getting the timing right. The glue must be tacky enough to attach the gold leaf but apply the metal layer too soon and it will trap moisture that will end up eating into the wood. Leave the delicate operation too late and there will be no sticking power left.

Will successfully applied gold leaf to the hands and the previously broken nose and toned down the newness of it. When all the angels had been buffed by a soft cloth, it was impossible to tell which had new hands or a nose job.

When they were returned to Gosberton Clough, parishioners were overwhelmed with the results.

'The angels are absolutely fantastic, far better than anything I imagined they could be,' said churchwarden Brian Tidswell.

His thoughts were echoed by David Dickinson who said: 'They have turned out so beautifully in this glorious gold colour. They are perfect, absolutely spot on.'

In addition to the congregation, Will won some unexpected backing from beyond the grave, from no lesser figure than the designer of the church, Sir Ninian Comper. His friend Betjeman leaves no doubt about how the eminent designer would have responded.

In Betjeman's words: 'His ecclesiastical tastes are rococo; he is perfectly satisfied so long as gold leaf is heaped on everywhere.'

A FOUNDLING'S TEDDY

I t seemed a winter's evening like every other as Mary busied herself in the basement kitchen of a shared Georgian house, waiting for husband John to return home for tea.

Outside, London was gloomy and pockmarked with bomb sites following the Blitz that had killed more than 20,000 people. As the Second World War had ended nine months previously, the outside air was no longer filled with the acrid smell of cordite from fallen explosives. Yet, chill nights like this one were still thick with pungent locomotive smoke drifting down from nearby King's Cross station.

A sharp rapping on the front door soon had Mary running upstairs, shivering a little as she parted company with her small coal fire in what would once have been the scullery of a fine house. Already she was aware it would not be anyone she knew well. Friends and relations used a single knock to bring her upstairs, while two knocks would fetch down the other residents in the house. This short volley of taps wasn't part of the household code.

At first, when she opened the door and looked right and left she saw no one. But as her eyes fell to the step, there was a brown paper carrier bag with string handles. Inside was a bundle of fabric. And suddenly the fabric moved.

Mary held her breath as she peered into the bag, now getting a better look at the baby inside. With a gasp, she swiftly picked up the bag, took it downstairs and, in the privacy of her home, she unwrapped a tiny girl, small enough to be a newborn. When John came home soon afterwards, he was stunned; first to hear the unfamiliar mew of a baby, then to see his wife cooing over the child, already smitten. Instantly he knew the baby wasn't newborn, but she was obviously undernourished. Together, their first instincts were good ones – to feed her and keep her warm.

The couple had met working in a munitions factory during the war. Having lost a leg after being run over in childhood, John wasn't able to join the armed services like other men his age. When they got married, he and Mary hoped nature would take its course and that a child would come along but nothing happened. As for all childless couples of the era, no explanation was given by doctors and none was sought.

Now, it seemed a miracle had happened. They had yearned for a baby and here one was, mysteriously delivered to their own front door. Together they emptied a drawer to use as a cot and rifled through their spare bedding to find the softest sheets. John shot out to a city centre chemist shop to buy formula milk and a bottle. Long after the baby nodded off to sleep with her belly full, they were wide awake in wonder at the evening's events and thrilled by the charms of unexpected parenthood.

The next morning dawned with creeping doubt. While the couple had already lost their hearts to this little lost soul, they were upright citizens and knew they would have to do the right thing. Now it was a case of fighting every instinct as Mary took the baby to the police station to give her up. A stern sergeant warned her she already risked arrest for not acting immediately.

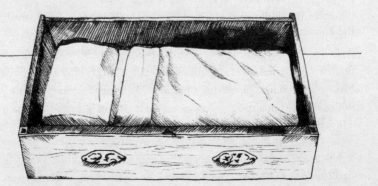

Next stop for the baby was an institution in Lewisham, where her mother came forward, not to claim her but to relinquish parental rights.

Here was more emotional turbulence for Mary and John, a glimmer of hope that the baby they had loved and lost in short order might rightfully be theirs. Still, they were warned she was so frail through malnourishment and gastroenteritis that she might yet not survive. The authorities now knew that she had been born in September, almost six months previously, but still only weighed 8lb.

Undaunted, they fostered her for several months until an adoption process was completed, naming their new daughter Lesley. One of the first gifts Mary bought her was a teddy bear, which became Lesley's life-long confidante, taking pride of place on her bed.

Almost 20 years later, when Lesley was about to get married and leave home, she realised her faithful companion Ted was looking a bit worse for wear. Cautiously, she set about him with some soap suds and a nail brush, then set him in front of the electric bar fire to dry. Distracted by something, she came back too late to save him from harm and Ted now had charred paws. She was distraught but couldn't face disposing of the ruined bear. Instead, she kept him in a bag for more than 50 years to stop him disintegrating before bringing him into the Repair Shop.

* * *

From the seventeenth century, the number of abandoned babies escalated, especially in London as the city became more crowded. In Europe, there were Catholic institutions to help deal with the issue, but Protestant England had rid itself of convents and the like during the Reformation. Also, illegitimacy was held in prurient disapproval, making the position of unmarried mothers almost untenable. According to Foundling Museum estimates, about 1,000 babies a year at the time were abandoned in London alone – on doorsteps, in churches or on rubbish heaps. The effect on mothers can only be guessed at, while the babies were vulnerable to disease and exploitation.

For philanthropic sea captain Thomas Coram, the pitiful situation seemed nothing short of a scandal. After he returned from America

Lesley with her mum Mary

in 1704 he set about rectifying this societal glitch, which was putting swathes of newborns at terrible risk, and spent 17 years lobbying for an establishment to be created that would help. He finally received a Royal Charter for the Foundling Hospital 'for the care and maintenance of exposed and deserted young children'.

It was more a haven than a hospital, offering refuge rather than a medical intervention. And even the term 'foundling' was used in its loosest sense. According to dictionary definition, a foundling is a baby that has been abandoned by its parents, often in a public place. However, at the Foundling Hospital mothers had to hand over their babies in person. This strict rule was suspended for a short spell from 1756 when a basket was hung on the gates so babies could be left anonymously. In response, the rates of mortality and baby trafficking leapt, so a line was drawn under this four-year trial and most mothers once again had to attend in person. One exception that held good for 50 years was that mothers of babies who came with a £100 donation could remain anonymous. About 75 babies came to the hospital under this rule before it too was stopped in 1801.

Since then, social provision has helped to reduce the numbers of foundlings, with contraception and welfare support two principal factors. Public attitudes to illegitimacy also mollified as the decades passed.

Yet the problem of abandoned babies hasn't gone away in the modern era. There have been two media reports – in 2012 and 2015 – that baby boxes or hatches were either being considered or had been installed in countries as diverse as China, Germany, Austria, Switzerland, Poland, the Czech Republic and Latvia, as well as the US state of Indiana. There have been calls for a similar system in the UK, where it's illegal to abandon a baby, although as many as 50 are left each year.

While baby boxes might well save the life of a discarded baby, the United Nations has come out against the policy as it almost irrevocably severs any opportunity of future contact between parent and child.

In childhood, life for Lesley was little short of idyllic. Although there wasn't much spare cash in the household, Lesley was the axis around which John and Mary's world pivoted. Those first few months of neglect were quickly put behind her as she thrived in the warmth of their uncon-ditional love.

The family moved out of the rented flat off Gray's Inn Road and went to Stoke Newington, with John managing a cleaning business.

At night, Lesley had a favourite fairy tale that she asked for again and again, so familiar to Mary that she needed no book to tell the story. 'Once upon a time, there was a man and a woman who longed for a baby and found a princess on their doorstep ...'

When she was six, the boy she was sitting next to at school spat out that Lesley was adopted. Distraught, she returned home and demanded that her mother explain. Gently, Mary pointed out that Lesley already knew the story of her babyhood off by heart as it had been told through the words of the familiar and enchanting night-time story on so many occasions. Lesley would never again be concerned about any perceived social stigma regarding adoption.

For her, it was nurture that trumped nature in her upbringing and anytime she referenced her mum and dad, she meant Mary and John. Her love and respect for the couple meant she would not seek the identity of her birth mother, at least not while they were alive.

Still, there were obvious signals that she came from different stock.

'Both my parents were very musical but even after piano lessons, I couldn't play a note,' she acknowledged. 'I was very artistic but neither of them could manage a convincing stick man!'

And there remained the nagging questions that every adopted child understands. Who are my genetic parents and what kind of life did they lead? Do I have brothers and sisters? Is there anyone out there who looks like me?

Today, DNA tests have helped to unlock the secrets of foundlings. Evolving computer technology has also thrown up some hacks in gene-alogy searches. Before that, for people like Lesley who wanted to know more, it was a case of trawling through archives.

She had a head start after her mum finally revealed the name of the woman on the adoption papers and the story she'd been told behind the desperate actions taken at the time.

Lesley as a young child with her parents

The woman – let's call her Sheila – was already pregnant for a second time when she left Lesley on the doorstep. Her story is complicated. Although she was married to someone in the Royal Navy, it seems Lesley's father was a Canadian, posted to London during the war. The new baby had another, different dad.

At the records office, Lesley discovered Sheila was divorced by her husband when it was acknowledged that neither child was biologically his. The painstaking search took Lesley, with a supportive colleague, through a paper trail of other marriages and divorces, until they finally discovered that Sheila had latterly been a resident of a warden-controlled home. As it turned out, they had uncovered this information just a short time after her death. However, together they paid a visit to the home to talk to people who knew her. And there on the wall was a photograph of Sheila. For Lesley, it was the curious sensation of looking in a mirror to the future, seeing an older woman who was outwardly a version of herself. Unexpectedly, the emotion was enough to put lead in her legs. Yet the moment quickly passed as she fell back on the security of her upbringing and found she could put her emotions in check.

Always guided by common sense and curiosity rather than the dead weight of emotional baggage, Lesley was so struck by her experiences that she later became an advisor to the adoption board of a London council.

Back at the Repair Shop, it was a case of returning Ted to his best life. To an uneducated gaze, he looked like an elderly bear, well-loved but worn out. For Lesley, he was an emblem of all the love that her mum and dad had lavished upon her from the moment she was left on their front step.

Bear ladies Julie and Amanda identified Ted as a Chiltern bear, made in Chesham, Buckinghamshire, during the 1940s, when bears made there started to carry an identifying label. Distinguishing features of a Chiltern bear are large, clear glass eyes with black pupils; a head stuffed with wood wool; cupped ears; long arms with spoon-shaped paws and silk-stitched claws.

The first task for the bear ladies was to open up the back seam and take out the body stuffing, which in repairs like this is almost always too historic to re-use. That Ted's chest fur was worn away by cuddles wasn't particularly a problem, but that threads of the fabric were being severed by the protruding edge of a growler inside was.

The growler now only emitted a tiny squeak and was duly dispatched to Steve Fletcher's work bench for repair, where he coated the bellows with rubberised paint to stop the leaks of air that were robbing Ted of his distinctive call. Established principles of conservation call for original parts to be redeemed wherever possible. As Steve pointed out, a brand new growler would have given the bear an entirely different character.

Amanda then removed the legs, emptied them and opened them out flat. It was time to wash the bear's empty body and leg fur and surface wash the arms and head which were still stuffed.

All stuffed toys gather dust, dirt or even acidic grit, which will eat away at the pile. Typically, the pair use a mild detergent, like baby shampoo – and then only the bubbles – in the washing process, wielding a flannel rather than scrubbing or rubbing. When it comes to drying the fur, it's not just Lesley's experience that has warned them against electrical drying devices. They always sit delicate and aged bear bodies on a towel to air dry.

Once dry, Amanda got to work on replacing the footpads, quickly realising it wasn't just the pads that had been singed but some of the adjoining fur as well. Having spatchcocked the leg, she saw what should have been a straight edge for a seam that would join the oval pad had been eaten away in places. Using tiny stitches, she attached a piece of colour-matched mohair fabric as a first step towards reinstating the damaged feet. She then made new paw pads out of a Rexine-style material – a piece of soft cotton, coloured with PVA and acrylic paint to give it a more traditional appearance. This time the material still looked too new, so it was rubbed with beeswax, a technique the bear ladies developed themselves during long experience of working on vintage bears.

The pads were set in before the legs were turned right side out. His new feet now looked in keeping with his original 'hands'. Julie lined the body with felt panels to strengthen and protect the aged fabric. Then she darned the area on the chest that had worn thin from the inside through close contact with the growler.

It was time to reunite Ted's head with his body. After Jay provided a bucket full of replacement kapok – silky fabric harvested from a tree – they got to work building up the bear again. It's not just a case of poking the kapok into flat limbs with fingers. Amanda and Julie have wooden-handled stuffing sticks for the task, pushing it into difficult-to-reach corners, twisting at the last to achieve a firmer finish.

It's important to get the amount of stuffing just right. Too much and there's new tension placed on old fabric, which will encourage holes. Too little and the bear's body will crease, which itself will weaken the fabric. Years of experience have informed the two when to stop as they repair stuffed toys. The finishing touches were the claw stitching, mimicking what would have been put in place decades ago by the manufacturers, and a pale blue ribbon around his neck.

A new future now awaited Ted as he would be put proudly on display in Lesley's home.

'Ted has been in a bag for the last 53 years because I was frightened of him falling apart,' Lesley explained.

'Today he is wonderful. You would never know that I had toasted him. My parents always knew Ted was my comfort blanket. They would be pleased that he can come out again where everyone can see what a wonderful little bear he is.'

A BLETCHLEY PARK BICYCLE

The bicycle was second-hand when it was given to her in 1937. To 18-year-old student Rachel Rawlence, it was much more than merely a set of wheels; she relished the liberty it gave her as she pedalled between lectures at Oxford University.

These were halcyon days. The horrors of the First World War, which ended a year before she was born, were now a faded memory and history scholar Rachel, in the city of dreaming spires, appeared to hold life with all its promise in the palm of her hand.

But black clouds were bubbling up on the horizon, as another colossal conflict positioned itself to engulf the globe. After three years bouncing across Oxford's cobbles, the bike's next duty was to transport Rachel around Bletchley Park, the stately home that had turned into a cipher centre, with its operations cloaked in secrecy. Later, the cycle carried Rachel with her children on a small attached saddle to the shops, and years after that, she was still using it to run errands.

Hardly surprising then that it was well worn when it arrived at the Repair Shop and there was plenty for expert Tim Gunn to fix. Apart from encroaching rust, the back brake rod was broken and the drive chain was stretched.

By now the bike meant much more to son Huw than just a vintage two-wheeled vehicle. Every spoke, sprocket and ting of the bell recalled his mother and her behind-the-scenes code-breaking work that helped end the Second World War. Yet, it's a puzzle that still had missing pieces.

Rachel was at the all-women St Hilda's College before joining Bletchley Park in 1941, where she worked as a cryptanalyst, a specialist in the analysis and decryption of enemy ciphers. But Huw has no idea how she was recruited. Some people were picked for their audacious ability at chess or crosswords; some were talented linguists or mathematicians; while others were friends of friends who already worked there. Much later, veterans recalled answering a knock on the door from a man in a dark suit, bowler hat and brolly, or even sending off a written application, ostensibly for a clerical role.

The aim of the job was to crack complex codes generated by Germany's Enigma machine, which so comprehensively scrambled words and phrases into gobbledegook that messages seemed impossible to unravel. But if Britain was to win the war, code breaking had to be carried out on an industrial scale.

Bletchley Park has had a variety of names, including the London Signals Intelligence Centre, Government Communications Headquarters, the Government Code and Cypher School, HMS *Pembroke V* or RAF Eastcote, Lime Grove or Church Green. People who worked there called it BP. As well as the mansion, there were a series of huts where specialists went to work.

Rachel joined in the same year that the men who ran BP made an urgent appeal to Prime Minister Winston Churchill for more resources. They told him that work he had previously deemed vital 'is being held up, and in some cases is not being done at all, principally because we cannot get sufficient staff to deal with it.'

A shortage of trained typists and the fatigue of decoding staff meant there was a critical backlog of work in Hut 6 in particular, a recently constructed wooden building on a brick plinth that dealt with military and air force signals. Instantly, Churchill responded by making BP a priority.

And it was to Hut 6 that Rachel was dispatched, 18 metres long and 9 metres wide, with two large rooms at one end and no toilets.

The task ahead for her and her BP colleagues across all the huts was immense, with an apparently endless number of coded messages fired off by the German army, navy and air force. Not only were the

Rachel during the Second World War

messages themselves of the utmost importance, but the conversations between operators were vital as 'traffic analysis' of salutations and idle chat about the weather could help break the code. Every letter and figure was captured by wireless intercept stations, the Y service, who duly dispatched them to Station X, yet another identity for BP.

Baffling though it might have seemed at this point, the information was recorded on index cards, which were duly made up into a catalogue for referencing.

Then the analysts got to work on fathoming the random selections from the alphabet made by the Enigma machines. Most commonly used in the war was the model Enigma 1, capable of 103,325,660,891,587,134,000,000 possible encryptions.

Enigma looked like an overblown typewriter with valves and electric circuitry, which had two keyboards and a plugboard that yielded lit-up letters, as well as three or five rotors to further mechanically scramble messages.

Its German operators were issued with sheets that told them how to align the settings, which rotors to use and which way to link up the plugboard. With this in hand, they could read incoming messages via the Enigma. The authorised settings were changed every 24 hours.

Five months before the outbreak of war, Poland's Cipher Bureau shared with its British and French counterparts the outcome it had achieved in breaking the Enigma codes; news that astonished the Allies. From that platform, Alan Turing, one of a top tier of cryptologists, statisticians and mechanical engineers at BP, expanded and progressed the Polish ideas until German Enigma codes could be broken. He designed the Bombe machines, which were able to automatically detect the Enigma 'keys', with each machine measuring an impressive 7 feet high and wide and weighing a ton. An idiosyncratic genius, who often chose to run 40 miles to meetings in London, Turing was an ideal candidate to steer the code-breaking operations. Logical and single-minded, as early as 1936 he had created a machine that could imitate thought and compute any number 'by rule of thumb', meaning it followed a due process.

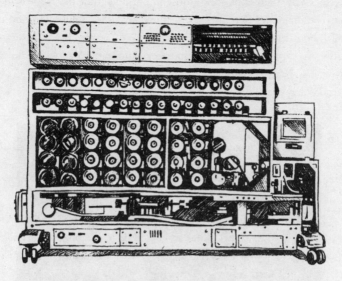

Installed in Hut 8, he focussed on the German naval codes. By the start of June, he could read the German code in real time – and not a moment too soon as the crisis of merchant shipping being sunk in the Atlantic was reaching its peak. The effect of this intelligence was so extraordinary that for the first 23 days of June the U-boats didn't sight a single convoy. Afterwards, British shipping could avoid the U-boat wolf-packs roaming the Atlantic and the net result was that Britain would not be starved into defeat.

But even with his know-how, combined with the lightning-fast wits of everyone who worked at BP, none of it was easy. For every victory in cracking a code, there were numerous failures. Even when messages were revealed, there were tough choices to be made as the British government went to elaborate lengths to hide the fact German codes could be read. If the enemy had been alerted, its own coding specialists might have shifted to a different scheme altogether, meaning the code-breakers would have to start from scratch again.

As a result, vital information from BP was smuggled into operations, paraded as something discerned by diplomats or spies.

Michael during the Second World War

Sometimes the Royal Navy, armed with secret information about an enemy convoy, might send a reconnaissance plane to its vicinity to explain why a submarine turned up shortly afterwards to sink ships.

Information culled by BP in Hut 6 proved pivotal in North Africa, where the action was see-sawing between the sides. Eventually, the British Eighth Army Commander Montgomery knew Rommel's every intention before it was executed on the battlefield. While campaigns still relied on boots on the ground, those front-line soldiers could now be used more intelligently by their commanders. BP also kept abreast of communications by the Italian armed forces and by the Japanese after Pearl Harbour catapulted them into the war in 1941.

The atmosphere in all the huts was tense. One woman confessed she was relieved to be moved from Hut 6's decoding room 'where all the operators were constantly having nervous breakdowns on account of the pace of work and the appalling noise'.

For Rachel, there was one upside that brightened even the darkest of days. This was in the shape of Stephen Michael Banister, a team leader in Hut 6 who worked at BP from 1939 after graduating as a classicist from King's College, Cambridge – the same college Turing had left five years earlier.

One of his major contributions was the 'Banister lists', known as Blists, containing enemy signals used in composing Bombe menus.

The couple wed in the spring of 1944, although Huw knows little of their courtship. Unlike other parents, Rachel and Michael, as he was known, didn't reminisce about the early days of their romance. It wasn't for a lack of sentimentality, more a rule of law. Both had signed the Official Secrets Act when they joined the ranks of BP workers and knew the pledge of silence they made held good for decades. Rachel, Michael and hundreds of other people linked to BP accepted a self-imposed Second World War amnesia to protect themselves from prosecution for spilling the beans about state secrets.

Some broadbrush facets of their BP existence are now known. Before their marriage they would have lived in lodgings around the town of Bletchley. The government had forbidden anyone else outside BP to billet there.

Most likely separately, or even as a couple, they would have visited the Bletchley Park Recreation Club, launched in October 1940 'to provide for all members of Bletchley Park facilities for recreation and amusements which otherwise do not exist ...' Costs were a shilling a month or 10 shillings a year, with squash, table tennis, drama, dancing and concerts among many pastimes on the agenda.

When Michael joined BP there were just 150 working there. At the end of the war, some 10,000 personnel worked in BP or at connected stations, three-quarters of which were women – and six out of ten of them were in uniform.

Hut 6 moved to Block D in February 1943. Within a year, the network at BP had achieved dominance over the Germans thanks to its code-breaking skills. Analysts could not only see what Germany's defence along the Atlantic wall looked like, but crucially also knew the top brass had swallowed the deception of 'Operation Fortitude', which made it seem as if the Allied invasion in 1944 was directed at Calais, rather than the Normandy Beaches.

However, any sense of triumph was contained among themselves as BP staff loyally observed the vow of stoical silence. Other service personnel who returned from the front line with a chest full of medals had plenty to say about their service, but BP workers remained mute, although they risked being thought of as shirkers or pen pushers in the process.

For those who did know of BP's existence, the message to its workers was unequivocal. General Dwight D. Eisenhower, Supreme Allied Commander, wrote: 'The intelligence which has emanated from you before and during the campaign has been of priceless value to me. It has simplified my task as a commander enormously. It has saved thousands of British and American lives ...'

Their work is thought by some to have shortened the war by two years and saved 14 million lives. Churchill referred to them as 'the geese that laid the golden eggs but never cackled'.

It was only in the 1970s that news about the work carried out at BP reached the public domain. Even then, Rachel and Michael found that being tongue-tied about their lives was a habit that was hard to break and they still didn't open up about their wartime service.

At the war's end, the expertise harnessed at BP was moved into an organisation now best known as Government Communications Headquarters, or GCHQ. Another result was the creation of Colossus, the world's first electronic computer.

On Rachel, the war left one noticeable scar. Huw recalls that throughout her life sudden loud noises or sirens made her agitated, possibly as a result of close calls in air raids.

Afterwards, she became a mother of four boys, which is when she used the bike to transport the youngsters on shopping trips, sitting on a small saddle in front of her own, safe between her arms. She continued to use the bike as a pensioner. Rachel died in 2019, six months after becoming a centenarian, living in the Surrey home that Huw grew up in almost until her death. Michael spent the rest of his working life with the Civil Service and died in 2006, aged 88.

The bike survived and even after being kept in a shed for a number of years, its original paintwork was relatively sound and the wheels were true.

Certainly, it needed a new saddle, with the existing one too dilapidated to salvage. Also, the rear sprocket had to be replaced as the teeth were too worn to effectively bite on the bike chain and power the rear wheel. For the moment it was held fast in its housing until Tim made a simple jig fixture to hold the sprocket and used an oxyacetylene torch to expand the thread. Finally, he brandished a chain whip to release the sprocket while it glowed cherry red with heat.

Fortunately, Tim had a replacement sprocket drawn from vintage stock with better-shaped teeth. This was cleaned and fitted back on the original hub.

Turning his attention to the broken rear brake rod, Tim knew the easiest option would be to fit a replacement. However, given the immense history of the bike, he decided to remove the rod and weld it back together

Rachel with one of her sons on the bike

Since the Repair Shop opened its doors, more than 30 experts have used their skills to fix treasured possessions that have come to the barn. The regulars include (l–r) Steve Fletcher, Julie Tatchell, Kirsten Ramsay, Amanda Middleditch, Will Kirk, Jay Blades and Lucia Scalisi.

Series presenter Jay Blades is a modern furniture restorer and upcycler with a passion for sustainability.

Originally, Court Barn, the home of *The Repair Shop*, stood for several centuries in Lee-on-Solent, Hampshire, before being moved to its present site in 1979.

Will Kirk's craftsmanship – which includes fixing fractured veneer, stopping table legs wobbling and making water marks disappear – was inspired by his woodworker grandfather and honed during a specialist course in antique furniture restoration at London Metropolitan University.

Steve Fletcher trained as an horologist, or clockmaker, following a family tradition in clockmaking that saw grandfather Fred using his talents during the First World War.

Bear ladies Amanda Middleditch and Julie Tatchell are not only empathetic repairers but experts at toy history too.

Working with malleable metals, silversmith Brenton West has a mix of ancient techniques at his disposal – a direct link to long-lost civilisations that have existed since the third century BC – as well as an array of modern technologies, which he studied at Medway College of Design.

Teamwork among the *Repair Shop* experts means they can draw from a deep well of experience when it comes to challenging restorations. As well as the regulars, such as Suzie Fletcher and Will Kirk (below), there are niche specialists, among them Roger Thomas, who fixes accordions, and John Dilworth, working with violins.

Years ago series presenter Jay Blades learned the restoration skills he uses in the barn from retired craftspeople during workshops he ran for young people. He is always keen to learn new techniques from his fellow experts, such as ceramicist Kirsten Ramsay.

Metalworker Dom Chinea has a background in graphic design and car restoration, as well as working as a set designer.

Ceramics expert Kirsten Ramsay trained at the renowned West Dean College and has 25 years' experience in restoration and conservation, including time spent working at the V&A and the British Museum.

Dom and Steve are both versatile craftsmen, able to turn their hand to a wide range of restorations. The *Repair Shop* team value each other's expertise and often work together to problem-solve on tricky fixes.

Along with programme viewers, Jay is keen to hear Will's detailed thought processes before another woodwork project is adeptly tackled.

Lucia Scalisi studied at the University of Northumbria and worked as a Senior Conservator of Paintings at the V&A before opening her own conservation studio in London.

Repair Shop experts are mindful of a natural tension between conservation – preserving something for the future while paying due respect to its past – and making an item robust and safe for future generations to enjoy.

Taking a break from their benches, the team step outside the barn, which is part of the Weald & Downland Museum, an outdoor museum devoted to disappearing aspects of rural life. Thanks to the demand for their different skills there can be up to a dozen people at work under the high wooden beams, as well as a visiting barn owl.

again. Of course, the bike would also benefit from some new tyres. After that, it was a case of reducing the bike to what Tim called 'component form' and cleaning every last nut and bolt before reassembling it.

Dom set about welding together the splits appearing in the mudguards, cautiously avoiding the sticker that showed the original provenance of the bike. It was made by the Birmingham Small Arms company, which began to manufacture bikes and bike parts in 1880.

Sharp-eyed Tim also spotted some flecks of white paint appearing on one small section on the back of the mudguards. It was, he explained, a square of white paint applied during the Second World War when lights on bicycles were illegal during a nationwide after-dark blackout. The white paint would be enough to alert other road users of the vehicle at close quarters.

For him, the extraordinary story of the bike was ingrained in its patina and through every worn part. On a test ride, he reflected on the role it had played and wondered how many other bicycles in Britain today are at once functional and mundane yet mysterious for the journeys taken.

For Huw, seeing the bike clean and in full working order was both emotional and nostalgic. For a moment, the days when he and his three brothers perched on the bike seemed only a heartbeat away.

A keen cyclist, Huw says the bike has three gears: high, higher and higher still. While his own sports bike weighs in at about 7.5 kilos, his mum's cycle weighs approximately 17 kilos and is built for someone slightly shorter than himself. Nonetheless, despite the effort needed, he uses it once a week up the winding drive of his Scottish loch-side home, carrying recycling in the wicker basket Tim put on and reflecting on this vintage workhorse, with its years of sterling service freely given to education and the nation, to children and for chores.

A CAPTAIN
SCOTT ALBUM

In a wind-lashed tent on a deserted continent, Captain Robert Falcon Scott lay bone-cold and statue-still in a sleeping bag, the dead bodies of two comrades in touching distance if only he had the strength to raise a hand. Years before he'd set off full of colonial confidence to claim the South Pole for the British Empire, but the mission had ended in disaster and his dreams were now white nightmares.

On 17 January 1912, Scott and his party had reached the Pole to find that they had been beaten by their Norwegian competitors by 33 days. His diary and letters, later recovered by a rescue team, are a window on his deteriorating outlook: 'The POLE. Yes, but under very different circumstances from those expected. Great God! This is an awful place and terrible enough for us to have laboured to it without the reward of priority.'

With a chronic shortage of supplies, Scott's men were hobbled by starvation, scurvy and hypothermia on the 800-mile return leg. To his wife, he wrote: 'You know I have loved you … quite the worst aspect of this situation is the thought that I shall not see you again – the inevitable must be faced.'

When a surviving trio decided against committing suicide, he made a closing diary entry: 'We shall stick it out to the end, but we are getting weaker, of course, and the end cannot be far. It seems a pity but I do not think I can write more.' In fact, his final words were a desperate plea: 'For God's Sake, look after our people.'

Noble, courageous and stoic, Captain Scott was dubbed a hero after news of his demise reached home shores, although infamous imperial

failures like this one were jarring for a society conditioned for triumph. But the expedition involved more than the five-strong team that perished, and many more words than this select few were written during the course of three years.

Although most people now recall it as a race to the Pole, there was a large body of scientific work carried out while Scott's ship, the *Terra Nova*, was anchored off Antarctica. The expedition included geologists, physicists, meteorologists and biologists, with some of the findings made there still current today.

Beyond that, there also exist two volumes of newspaper clippings from the era that show just how the Antarctic expedition had captured public interest. They were commissioned by Isobel Paterson, who'd met and fallen in love with Henry Rennick, the handsome hydrographer on Scott's crew. At the time, newspaper readers were captivated not only by the adventurous tale but also by the dramatic images, as photographer Herbert Ponting was on the team. Ponting also kept a film diary of the expedition from its beginning, at a time when silent movies were still a novelty.

In the *Standard* on 12 October 1910, there's a report of a screening of 3,000 feet of footage by Ponting, which had been recently received from Antarctica to the gasps of expedition backers and a proud public. The description was published with the headline 'Vivid Record'.

In a cosy little darkened room just off Piccadilly Circus last evening a special company of about forty persons sat and watched a small band of men fighting their way over mountains of ice towards the South Pole ...

Down go the lights and flash on the screen comes the picture of the brave little Terra Nova gliding out of port. On beach and pier crowds of people wave their adieus – one can almost imagine one hears the shouts – and gradually the shore fades out of view and the scene is changed to life on board the stout little ship.

Pictures are given of the adventurers preparing dinner, feeding the dogs and Lieutenant Rennick is seen playing the barber to Dr Wilson [who would later die in the tent, next to Scott].

On December 9 an immense iceberg approached the vessel – so near that it towered above the craft to an alarming extent as it sailed majestically on its way northwards.

A photograph appeared in the *Daily Mirror* on 11 May 1911, with officers and scientists at dinner on the ship with a teddy bear mascot on the table. 'The quality of the picture, its clearness and repleteness of detail is a testimony to the skill of the photographer Mr H G Ponting,' said the accompanying report. 'Hitherto all polar photographs have been taken by amateurs but Mr Ponting's professional experience and "touch" is clearly seen here.'

In subsequent decades, Isobel read and re-read the words that charted the expedition's course and gazed longingly at the pictures, both tangible touching points with the man she loved. For while Henry would return from the icy depths of the Antarctic, he would not survive the imminent war. Likewise, her family pored over the clippings until the pages were well-thumbed and both spines were splitting.

In this well-handled condition, the pair of volumes arrived at the Repair Shop for the attention of bookbinder Christopher Shaw. Henry Rennick's granddaughters Jenny and Patricia were concerned that the clippings would not weather another generation. Said Jenny: 'The books hold such incredible importance to us. We never knew our grandfather, so these albums are the closest item the family has to hearing the accounts of his expedition first hand.'

Henry Edward de Parny Rennick was born in India in 1881, the son of a British army colonel who died when Henry was eight years old. He enrolled in the Royal Navy aged just 14, studying at Britannia Royal Naval College and passing out as a Midshipman, just as Scott had done a dozen years previously.

Henry served on numerous ships, including *Warspite* and *Dreadnought*, working his way through the ranks until he was a Lieutenant Commander.

Meanwhile, Scott had already captured the interest of many adventurers with an earlier government-funded expedition to Antarctica on the ship *Discovery*, just after the turn of the twentieth century.

The prize of being first to reach the South Pole remained, and Scott masterminded plans for another mission to capture it for Great Britain. But this time there was a shortage of cash; of the £40,000 needed, the Government had only provided half, while a further £14,000 had been raised by public subscription.

Although he was wrestling with an absence of funds this time, Scott had no shortage of volunteers, with 8,000 men signalling their interest. Rennick was one of 70 men picked for the *Terra Nova* ship, which steamed out of Cardiff on 15 June 1910 at the start of a three-year odyssey. As the coastline slipped out of sight, none onboard knew how much inner resilience and iron will each would need as they confronted the brutal realities of deadly weather.

Freezing temperatures and howling gales make Antarctica the most inhospitable place on Earth. Temperatures in the summers average at minus 27.5°C, while in the winter that figure plummets to minus 60°C.

Henry Rennick and fellow crew members

Henry Rennick with a penguin

Meanwhile, the wind can gust up to 150mph and Scott's polar dash was to be hampered by unseasonal blizzards that year.

At about 50 times the size of Great Britain, the continent had until then been the domain of lumbering seals, screeching seabirds and five varieties of penguins.

It's likely Henry initially aspired to be among the shore parties, heading off on the ice into the unknown depths of Antarctica, treading where no human boot had been before. This was heady stuff in the heroic age of polar exploration.

But during his time in the navy, Henry had been a boxer and a thorough medical examination after one bout revealed a heart murmur; not bad enough to end his career, but something that barred him from the extraordinary exertions of polar hikes.

Instead, Henry had been assigned the job of hydrographer, plotting features below the surface of the sea and taking soundings. Even staying on the ship or close to the shore, as Henry did, meant enduring icy temperatures and he must have been awed by the hostile terrain.

Scott took ponies and dogs to propel the Pole expedition team across the ice, while Roald Amundsen – the Norwegian who mounted a rival unannounced expedition to lay claim to the South Pole – focussed only on dogs. Inclement weather hindered the dumping of supplies intended for the return leg. Alongside Scott's final expedition, there were numerous others that began from the *Terra Nova*, heading to hitherto unknown areas to search and survey mountains, coastlines and crevasses. Indeed, while Scott's party was missing, another group was also unaccounted for, after a planned 55-week expedition lasted almost twice as long following a missed rendezvous. They spent the second unscheduled winter in an ice cave lined with seaweed, eating seal meat and blubber along with a few biscuits, cocoa and sugar, then trekked for 200 miles to reach the safety of the ship.

After the weather relented, a party went to find the bodies of the missing men. One sombre newspaper clipping explains what happened next: 'Surgeon Atkinson … gathered the records and the effects of the dead men, read the burial service over their bodies and erected a cairn and cross to their memory over the inner tent in which they buried them.'

In January 1913, the *Terra Nova* left Antarctica, reaching New Zealand a month later when a telegram was sent to Britain relaying the terrible news.

For Henry, it had been a transformative trip. He left his mark on the region, not least as one of the largest glaciers on the continent, at some 320km long, was named for him, as was a bay leading from it.

And it was life-changing for personal reasons as, after the ship docked in New Zealand en route to Antarctica, he had met Isobel, the daughter of a New Zealand businessman with Scottish heritage, from Dunedin.

Keeping clippings from newspapers in scrapbooks was common at the time to keep track of people or places. However, it's clear Isobel was a young woman of some means as she asked a London-based service to monitor press coverage of the *Terra Nova* so she would have access to every morsel of information. It meant the chunky tomes were bound in leather and tooled in gold leaf.

Although the expedition ended disastrously, Henry returned to New Zealand to propose to his newfound love.

As they married in Westminster, London, in April 1914, the volumes probably served as a wedding gift. In it were weighty reminders of the expedition's fatal result.

With the headline 'What Is the Good of It', one clipping sums up the national feeling like this:

> In the grief and pity with which the deaths of Captain Scott and his companions have stirred every bosom and in the wonder at heroism which went so simply and so patiently to its death every other feeling is lost.
>
> It is impertinent to ask whether there is not here a waste of heroism and nobility; it seems almost sacrilege to inquire since the men who died were satisfied to give their lives for the objects they pursued, whether the objects themselves were worth it.

According to the *Daily Graphic:* 'In all our records there is nothing to surpass the prolonged struggle and courageous death of Captain Scott and his comrades.' It was the nation's duty to provide for the families of the dead men, the newspaper insisted, and 'the shillings of the poor and the pounds of the rich will be given with eagerness'. It was like an answer to Scott's final exhortation: his people would indeed be looked after by the nation.

The *Daily Mail* shone a light on Scott's character, which offered an inkling of Henry's own experience of him: '[Scott] was a born leader of men; iron in his discipline but with a singular power of evoking sympathy and affection. Thus he was followed with zeal and he commanded a veritable band of brothers.'

There was also widespread acknowledgement of the scientific advancement the expedition had brought about:

> We now know that the South Pole is covered by a great land surface like a cap … science may learn from the details of this distribution of land and sea masses at the Poles something fundamentally important about the flow of ocean currents, which are profoundly influenced by these Polar regions and by the way in which the earth's waters flow about them.

Although the expedition had ended the previous year, Henry spent months writing up his findings, a task he finally completed in June 1914.

Two months later, it seemed clear Britain would soon be at war. Before hostilities were officially declared, Henry had joined the cruiser HMS *Hogue* as a Navigating Officer.

Launched in 1900, the *Hogue* and her sister ships *Aboukir* and *Cressy* were disappointing performers from the get-go and were now at war with a scratch crew and travelling at slower speeds than ever. With the three ships bunched together on patrol, old naval hands nicknamed the group the 'Live Bait Squadron'.

Their task was to watch the entrance to the English Channel, but each vessel's lack of agility and speed meant they weren't zigzagging as they should have to evade submarine attack. Perhaps it was complacency that led them to believe there were no submarines in the area, but in any event, the threat from U-boats didn't loom large at the time.

Unseen, the prowling, primitive U-9 had spotted the trio through its periscope. After submarine Captain Otto Weddigen fired a torpedo at 06.25 on the morning of 22 September, it was first thought the *Aboukir* had hit a mine. Its Captain beckoned the other two ships in to help pick up survivors, inadvertently lining them up for the submarine's next attack.

Hogue was next to be hit, from a range of just 300 yards. With its lifeboats already committed to the water, the only option for those aboard was to leap into the water.

Henry had the presence of mind to grab a life jacket before jumping, but in the waves he saw a colleague who was a father, struggling to keep his head above water. Immediately, Henry thrust the buoyancy aid at him, imploring him to take it for the sake of his children.

It took only ten minutes for *Hogue* to sink. As she was disappearing below the water, *Cressy* was torpedoed and in those moments of chaos and dread, with oil spills on the water and the shrieks of terrified men filling the air, Henry was dragged to his death beneath the waves. Altogether, 1,459 men from all three ships perished that morning, a major disaster for the Royal Navy just seven weeks after the start of the First World War. Although submarine warfare was in its infancy, its threat could no longer be underestimated.

In later press reports, Henry was lauded as a hero for his actions that morning. Tragically, he didn't know he was going to become a father himself as Isobel was four months pregnant. At 23, she was a widow and a mother-to-be and tortured with grief, so much so that her dark, coiffed hair turned snow-white overnight.

The volumes now assumed far greater importance, as a link to Henry for both herself and their son John. Until this day, Jenny and Patricia had been reluctant to entrust the family record to anyone for repair.

In *The Repair Shop* barn, Jenny met bookbinder Chris Shaw, who is a Fellow of Designer Bookbinders. For the last 35 years he's covered all aspects of binding, from cloth and leather, to box making and restoration, although his life could have been very different. He admits he wasn't an accomplished academic at school. 'So it was either the Foreign Legion or bookbinding. And I was too short for the Foreign Legion.'

For him, each job is unique, and not just because of the extent of the repairs needed. Connected to every project is a story that unfolds with twists and turns. This tale he found particularly absorbing.

Keen to showcase his craft, he had a three-stage plan to refurbish the volumes; firstly dismantling each book, then re-lining the spine and finally replacing the damaged section of the cover with new goatskin.

Using a scalpel, he removed the ribbed leather covering on the spine and the boards that formed its front and back. Then he added one layer of strong, stiff calico and several of strong kraft paper to the spine, using reversible PVA glue, to introduce new strength at its core. These would be the new hinges of the thick inside boards that bear the cuttings.

Rebacking is the term for repairing a spine with new material, whether it is on a cloth, leather or vellum binding, but the new addition won't necessarily be apparent. Chris always aims to preserve and remount the original spine piece to conserve the book's appearance.

This time, the rebacking was initially hidden by a new goatskin cover. In turn, that was obscured by the original spine, severed at the start of the repair. It meant the 120-year-old lettering – which read 'British Antarctic Expedition 1910' – remained on display. After all the layers on the spine were glued into place, the book was wrapped up like a mummy and left overnight so there was no opportunity for slippage.

To disguise the joins and mask wear and tear on the board covers, Chris gently daubed on a dye. Both covers were then sealed with wax, making 110-year-old leather look like new.

It was, Chris assured Jenny, a 'belt and braces' job, so the volumes would last for many more generations keen to read of the heroic exploits and the key role their ancestor played in one of history's most epic tales.

AN AIRMAN'S JACKET

P oking up through the Atlantic rollers, the Azores are volcanic and verdant, with views to the horizon unencumbered by any distant shores. These nine islands, with high peaks and azure lagoons, stand remotely in the Atlantic Ocean, some 800 miles off the coast of Portugal. In peacetime they serve as a tranquil bolt-hole for holidaymakers. During the Second World War, the islands were a prize with such strategic value that both Britain and Germany had plans to seize the Portuguese colony by force.

Although Portugal's ruler, Salazar, was a Fascist, he had no love for Germany, fearing Hitler planned to invade the Iberian peninsula. Meanwhile, British politicians pondered whether a long-standing Anglo-Portuguese treaty would hold fast in such a tumultuous political climate. In 1943, Britain – with America standing at its shoulder – asked if it could lease the islands to help patrol the Mid-Atlantic Gap. Portugal said yes.

That's how the men of the Royal Air Force Coastal Command found themselves in an idyllic location, confronting a wartime task unlike any other. Among the men who served there was Londoner Harry Lofting and it was his flying jacket that found its way to the Repair Shop, with grandson John cradling it in his arms. Harry's long war service, reflected in the wear and tear on the jacket, relates the rarely told story of Coastal Command.

By the outbreak of the Second World War, the Royal Air Force had been split into three sections. Fighter Command was at the forefront during the Battle of Britain in 1940 when its pilots and planes fended off incoming Luftwaffe bombers. As the conflict progressed, Bomber Command gained prominence in monumental raids carried out against Germany and its allies to obliterate their industrial might. As for Coastal Command, its activities during the Battle of the Atlantic went below the radar for most people, when in fact it was in action from the first day of the conflict until its very end and its role was decisive.

As Germany appeared to gain the upper hand in the spring of 1940, the men of Coastal Command patrolled the British coastline, looking for sea or airborne intruders. While the threat of invasion receded, the peril of prowling U-boats did not, and it was Coastal Command's job to pick them off from the skies. And to stop Britons starving, their planes also protected transatlantic convoys bringing raw materials and food to Britain. In addition, the planes harried enemy vessels, laid mines, acted as minesweepers, searched for downed airmen and did reconnaissance. Sometimes these tasks overlapped with the Fleet Air Arm, the Royal Navy's flight wing, which had planes taking off from aircraft carriers to meet the enemy.

In news reports of the era, Coastal Command airmen were heralded as 'sky sentries on patrol'. Yet on the ground, it was often treated as the service's poor relation. While Britain was being squeezed by Luftwaffe and U-boat activities, there's no doubt that the maritime air forces were sidelined in the competition for scarce resources, at least for the first few years of the war.

Arguments for defending trade routes as a priority put by both Coastal Command and the Fleet Air Arm failed to land with the government for some time. By 7 September 1941, Winston Churchill acknowledged Coastal Command 'was particularly hard hit by the cuts which we were forced to make in its expected scale of expansion'. (He said his job was to 'fight on all the administrative fronts at once,' and, 'amid conflicting needs', find the right solution.)

The strength of Coastal Command was also depleted in favour of the 1,000 bomber raids planned over Germany from 1942. In September that year, two Coastal Command squadrons were assigned to Bomber Command.

Yet, until the end of 1942, the Germans were sinking ships faster than the British could build them. That year alone, nearly eight million tonnes of shipping was destroyed in the shape of 1,664 ships and their cargo – two-thirds of it by U-boats. Coastal Command crews were based around the UK until bases opened in Iceland, Gibraltar and West Africa, as well as the Azores. That amounted to a staggering 10 million square miles of ocean that needed patrolling. As both sides raced towards technological superiority, Coastal Command crews played a cat-and-mouse game with their U-boat prey.

Thanks to the way they were powered, U-boats couldn't stay submerged for long. Royal Navy ships were armed with sonar, which could detect a submarine on the ocean floor, while patrolling aircraft were watchful from the skies. Accordingly, German submarines developed a habit of staying below the waves by day and coming up at night, when they could make hastier progress.

Coastal Command aircraft carried night-and-day kit to detect surfaced vessels at sea, called Air-to-Surface radar. Although it picked out an object in endless miles of open sea, the target dropped off the radar as the plane homed in. In daylight when the plane inevitably circled to line up its fire, any pinpointed submarine had time to dive. At night, the pursuit of submarines seemed near impossible, with the use of flares offering patchy coverage as the U-boat sank from view. Soon a powerful spotlight was attached to the underside of Coastal Command planes to better illuminate the targets, called a Leigh Light, and that helped.

But in the autumn of 1942, German U-boats were fitted with special receivers that picked up the radar signals, and could once again dive before the aircraft reached the target. As a result, Coastal Command successes in sinking U-boats declined and losses in merchant shipping increased. Sightings of U-boats in 1942 declined from 120 in September to 57 in October.

The situation was reversed only when Bomber Command reluctantly handed over the new H2S apparatus that operated on short wave and was thus not detectable by German crews.

Harry and Jeanette on their wedding day

In time, Coastal Command was also able to piggyback on German position-finder beams established in northwest Spain and the French Atlantic coast and intended for use by German pilots, to confront incoming Luftwaffe aircraft.

After the war started, Harry left his job as a clerk to join up at RAF Padgate in Lancashire and he was ideally placed to observe every ebb and flow in the fortunes of Coastal Command. His route through the service isn't entirely clear, although his training as a wireless operator is recorded. But it is known that he married his sweetheart Jeanette in 1943 within a few days of becoming a flying officer.

He'd won his wings at a critical time, with Coastal Command taking delivery of improved long-range aircraft from America to expand their range across the Atlantic. For U-boats, it was now a case of the hunter becoming the hunted. But this was no turkey shoot. Given the breadth of the ocean and the limited size of their cautious target, patrols were tedious and at the same time an exhausting test of endurance.

After his wedding, Harry was sent to the Azores, where crews became accustomed to hot sunny days, Saharan winds and exotic flowers. Still, it was no summer holiday as flying routines outlined in logbooks now stored at the National Archives reveal. They relate long and often fruitless patrols across the open ocean, with the crew members straining their gaze, effectively looking for periscopes breaking the surface. Instead, they were more likely to see empty life rafts, isolated oil slicks or dead whales. Yet, no matter how many hours they were in the sky during this humdrum vigil, out of sight of land, ships or other aircraft, the crew couldn't afford to let concentration levels lag for a moment.

On 1 August 1944, for example, five patrols left the Lagens base on the Azores, flying more than 65 hours between them, with the longest being airborne for more than 13 hours. None of the five had anything to report.

The following day a patrol reported: 'Radar contact made but disappeared. Flares released but nothing seen and contact not regained. Operator certain that contact was of a heavy rain cloud.'

And there was always the shadowy fear of ditching in the sea, hundreds of miles from land. One patrol that left Lagens that month suffered a starboard engine failure nearly nine hours into the flight. 'Base informed and depth charges were jettisoned. Position reported to base every 15 minutes until landing safely at 22.06.' That was 12 hours after take-off.

By the end of the month, crews had spent 1,248 hours in the air on 98 different sorties. But they had nothing to inscribe on to the side of their cockpits by way of a kill. Even when crews carried out attacks, there was often no way of being sure they had scored a hit.

One log entry following an encounter recounted: 'No oil or air bubbles seen but patch of white substance was observed at time of attack alongside a swirl and after attack this swirl broke up in several streaks, spreading as if coming up from below.'

A film made about Coastal Command in 1943 by the government's propaganda unit, with a rousing soundtrack by Ralph Vaughn Williams, revealed how men onboard passed the time by puffing on pipes and drinking tea as they took turns on watch.

Churchill called the Battle of the Atlantic 'the dominating factor of the war' but understood the moments of glory were rare. He wrote: 'for the individual sailor or airman in the U-boat war there were few moments of exhilarating action to break the monotony of an endless succession of anxious, uneventful days. Vigilance could never be relaxed. Dire crisis might at any moment flash upon the scene with brilliant fortune or glare with mortal tragedy. Many gallant actions and incredible feats of endurance are recorded but the deeds of those who perished will never be known.'

But with better science on their side in the form of the code-breakers of Bletchley Park, Coastal Command in concert with the Royal Navy began to win the war waged with U-boats. In March and April 1943, 27 U-boats were destroyed in the Atlantic alone, more than half by air attack. In May alone, 40 U-boats were sunk.

During those long hours spent in the sky, with just fellow crew members for company, it's hardly surprising that men's minds would wander, often into the fanciful. That was always the case when the mission met unexpected hitches and the blame was put squarely on gremlins.

Harry in uniform

These impish creatures of an unknown realm were blamed for fuel loss, jammed radio frequencies, sand in fuel pipes, severed wires, torn tyres, broken windows, and incessant and inexplicable knocking sounds inside the fuselage.

At one stage in the war, Harry found himself dumped in the sea after problems with his aircraft. It seems likely he blamed gremlins for the monumental event because that's what he named his family home in later life. At the end of the war, Harry served with 280 Squadron, based at Thorney Heath, and was in its ranks until it was disbanded in the summer of 1946.

In his time in the RAF, he worked in or alongside Beauforts, Manchesters, Wellingtons, Catalinas, Flying Fortresses and others. Thousands of feet in the air, he and the rest of the crew relied on their flying jackets for protection in the primitive cockpit against biting cold. They had all been issued with waist-length flying jackets designed by American aviator Leslie Irvin, who also invented a rip-cord parachute system. Each one was made with supple leather for ease of movement and thick sheepskin to provide insulation. A wide, lined collar could be up-turned for further warmth and there was a belt at the waist to main-tain a snug fit. Any dip in the pilot's body temperature could result in a treacherous lapse in concentration. For Coastal Command alone, a fluorescent yellow hood was attached to more easily identify someone ditched in the ocean. The jacket's production centre during the war was Letchworth, Hertfordshire.

John left the jacket at the Repair Shop, apprehensive about staging a surprise for his father Graham. There had been surreptitious plotting by John with Graham's wife Helen to get access to the jacket. What would Graham's reaction be when it was fully refurbished? Suzie had appre-hensions of her own, about a hole in the shoulder and the task of replac-ing the zips.

But her first task was to hand sew the seams, where original thread that had held each heavy section in place for decades was giving way. Given the thickness of the jacket's sheepskin, these had to be overstitched by hand, which was a physically demanding task. A saddler by trade, Suzie is no stranger to sewing cumbersome items, but nonetheless, it was a demanding fix. The biggest challenge was the armpit seams, where three panels met in short order, at difficult angles.

Then she had to reattach strips of leather that overlayed the seams, most of which had come away as, again, the original stitching was rotten. She had an ally, her Singer sewing machine called Pearl, one of 2,000 industrial sewing machines made in 1951 and operated by handle and treadle. Matching each new stitch to the hole made by its predecessor, she combined Pearl's sedate pace and unremitting power to her advan-tage as she wrestled the bulky jacket beneath the machine's foot.

It was now the shoulder hole that needed her attention. She began by cutting away the wool on the inside that surrounded it, so the previ-ously covered leather was revealed. Then she took a square of lined aviator leather to stabilise the frayed edges. Both the newly revealed leather sections and the smooth surface of the patch were covered in adhesive. Working steadily, Suzie pushed the patch into place from the inside, giving her a surface on which to bond flaking pieces, keeping the appearance as authentic as possible.

Although it wasn't the original zip, the one in the jacket had lost a selection of teeth. When she took the replacement zip apart she double-checked that she didn't get the sides mixed up and end up with the slider on the inside of the jacket before starting the connecting seam.

The jacket had a chain at its collar for hanging. But the leather had torn here too and had to be replaced. Vintage jackets like this one should be hung on a hanger or mannequin, rather than by a loop, Suzie explained.

Cleaning the leather was a cautious process as age had rendered the surface scaly and cracked and she didn't want to inadvertently remove ageing flakes. She conditioned the elderly leather as well before a final clean with saddle soap.

All the while, she was thinking about men like Harry who had worn the jacket in combat, only to find themselves weighed down by it if they were pitched into the sea.

'When I researched the Coastal Command I was shocked at how little training these young men had and the lack of support! They also had sheepskin dungarees so it's a wonder they were able to float with that weight of wet sheep skin.'

Helen, Graham's wife, who works for the Willows and Wetlands Centre, lured him to the Repair Shop on the pretence of an awards ceremony for visitor attractions.

As Graham saw John and Mick at the barn, his face lit up. Yet still, he had no idea of what was to come.

When the jacket was unveiled, John's head swivelled towards his father. Any concerns fell away as Graham focussed wordlessly on one of the few remaining links he had with a father who was gone from his life at an early stage. Harry worked for the government-run betting outfit the Tote until he died in 1968 in his mid-fifties and when Graham was still a teenager. The loss was keenly felt by Graham and brother Mick. For Graham, there would be no opportunity to chat about his dad's wartime heroics over a pint in the pub. In any case, Harry – like many men of his generation and experience – had a natural reticence when it came to talking about his experiences.

As well as finding out more about a grandfather he never knew, John had plotted the surprise as he holds Graham in such high esteem. For his part, Graham had treasured the flying jacket as one of the few mementos he had of a valiant man he never knew well. The jacket also symbolised the courage of all the men of Coastal Command. During the Second World War, Coastal Command had a million airborne hours to its credit, carrying out 240,000 operations, destroying 212 U-boats and 366 German transport vessels. In notching up these statistics, 2,060 aircraft were lost and nearly 6,000 men died.

When it came to taking back the jacket, Graham decided that son John would now be the custodian. Suzie held her breath for a moment, praying the jacket would fit and the zip would work. Thankfully, the sizing was perfect. Said Graham: 'We have been brought together by a simple piece of clothing. If we look after the jacket it will be a focal point to reflect on these people who are no longer with us, but with us in thought.'

The sight of the jacket made Mick 'humble and proud'.

A LANTERN CLOCK

In the seventeenth century, pendulum clocks were cutting-edge technology, something similar to artificial intelligence today. For centuries, people had told the time using the sun or a sundial, sand and sometimes water.

Medieval clocks were the first mechanical timepieces, with weights and gears to pace the passing hours, but they were notoriously inaccurate, as were clocks operated by springs and balance wheels. It wasn't until the metronomic qualities of the pendulum were realised that Europe became time-precise.

The oldest item ever to reach *The Repair Shop* work benches was a lantern clock that predated pendulums. It was ticking before Britain's population was decimated by bubonic plague and prior to the Great Fire of London. The protruding teeth on the cogs inside were painstakingly ground out by hand when England was still reeling from a civil war that had torn families and friends into opposing camps – which then fought to the death.

A lantern clock is named for its shape and has an outsized face, fretted brass work, exposed working parts and a domed hood to provide the chime. At a distance of almost four centuries, it's impossible to say with certainty just what this clock looked and sounded like when it was made, but there was definitely just one hand, denoting the hours, rather than two like today, and a series of balance wheels to make it function, instead of a pendulum.

Lantern clocks like these were being built on the cusp of a clock-making revolution, and later a pendulum was installed to enhance its accuracy. It bore the name of the clockmaker, Thomas Loomes, one of a select few in business at the time. It's thought all his lantern clocks were originally made with the kind of balance-wheel controls that were soon to give way to pendulums.

Owner Frank Black recalled being mesmerised by the clock as a child and, himself an engineer, he has branded early clockmakers like Loomes 'miracle workers' for the exquisite mechanical parts they harmonised in the body of timepieces.

Despite its great age, the clock had been working until about 70 years ago when it was taken out of its long case, which had become riddled with woodworm. For safekeeping, it was put into a cardboard box bearing the name 'Monk & Glass 10 Minute Pudding', the packaging of a custard-making company run by Wilfred Monkhouse, father of British comedian Bob.

'It always felt it was a crying shame to have a clock such as that sat in a box under the stairs, doing nothing,' said Frank. 'It is something special, a piece of history.'

Since then, the added pendulum and weights had been parted from the clock. But that did nothing to diminish the excitement of horology expert Steve Fletcher.

Instantly, he could solve one of the clock's enduring mysteries. On the bottom, the year 1620 had been engraved by an unknown hand when Thomas Loomes, whose name appeared further up, wasn't born until at least six years after that.

It was an example of historical recycling, Steve explained. The outer body of one clock made at that earlier date was potentially reused by Loomes, probably when it was being updated as technology evolved. A glance into the housing revealed other alterations had been carried out down the centuries. Just like a house, the clock had been modernised with new additions installed to replace worn-out working parts. As a chunky hand-cut screw from the clock rolled around the palm of his hand, Steve pondered the way the world had been nearly four centuries ago, when this scrap of metalwork was made.

As it happens, the life of Thomas Loomes gives sharp definition to a distant era, when faith and politics were distilled into a toxic combination.

Frank's grandfather Robert Black – the earliest
known owner of the clock – with his family

Loomes was born just as the reign of Charles I was getting underway, with squabbles between Parliament and the monarch already evident. Charles, with his Scottish accent and stammer, was a patron of the arts and a fan of hunting. But he was rarely seen by his subjects, and people suspected him of Catholic sympathies when the country was Protestant by inclination.

Unrest in both Scotland and Ireland compelled him to seek the financial assistance of Parliament. But nothing could fig-leaf his dearly held authoritarian principles, as he repeatedly dissolved the House of Commons and asserted that he had a God-given right to rule.

Rising tensions finally erupted into Civil War in 1642, with the country divided between Cavaliers, who supported the King, and Roundheads, who backed Parliament.

Among the most brutal of conflicts, this civil war claimed the lives of 85,000 soldiers. The execution of the King in January 1649 didn't end the fighting, and a further 100,000 people are thought to have died from war-related disease with bloody disturbances rumbling on into 1652.

Farmer-turned-soldier Oliver Cromwell came to prominence in civil war clashes, chiefly for having well-organised and loyal troops that repeatedly triumphed against Royalist forces. Having put his name to the King's death warrant, Cromwell went on to brutally crush rebellion in Ireland before starting a period of rule in Britain.

Motivated by Puritan zeal, Cromwell himself began dissolving Parliament when its members didn't concur with his views and was finally anointed Lord Protector, so was king in all but name. Long after peace was restored, society remained split.

The engraving on the clock front confirms that Loomes worked at premises known as the Mermaid in Lothbury, an area of London that had long been associated with metalworking.

In the first half of the seventeenth century, there were just a few master clockmakers at work there with a number of apprentices signed up to them to learn the trade. At the time, industry in the City of London was controlled by a number of guilds and clockmaking was no exception. In 1631, the Clockmakers' Company began, ostensibly so artisans could unite to fend off foreign competition. Soon the aim was to stop clockmakers working unless they were signed up and limit the scope of their work even if they were.

Loomes was an apprentice with William and John Selwood, makers of lantern clocks. In 1649, he became a brother of the Clockmakers' Company, just weeks before Charles I was beheaded at Whitehall. The Selwoods both died young, which left Loomes unexpectedly in charge of an established workshop in 1653. He was not yet 30, a fact likely to cause envy among rivals.

Moreover, the Clockmakers' Company had Royalist sympathies, while Loomes was known for his active support of Parliamentarians.

When Loomes married the following year, it was to Mary Fromanteel, whose father Ahasuerus was a clockmaker in Southwark and had the same religious and political mindset as Loomes. The couple had a daughter, also called Mary, in 1655. Loomes and Ahasuerus were potent and ambitious allies.

When Ahasuerus sought to sidestep the trading restrictions of the Clockmakers' Company, he asked Cromwell himself to make him a freeman of the City of London. In 1656, the Lord Protector duly obliged.

There followed some tit-for-tat spats between Loomes, backed by Fromanteel, and the Clockmakers' Company. At one stage, Loomes gathered a petition of names objecting to the Clockmakers' Company admitting Frenchmen and presented it to London's Lord Mayor. He was

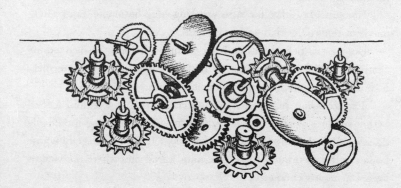

subsequently prosecuted by the Clockmakers' Company for having more than the requisite number of apprentices.

But the political ground was shifting beneath their feet. First Cromwell withdrew from public life, then he became ill and died. Clockmakers Fromanteel and Loomes must have felt the chill wind of change, yet the older man still had an ace card to play. In 1656, scientist and philosopher Christiaan Huygens from the Netherlands built the first pendulum clock. Within two years, Fromanteel had won from him an agreement to sell pendulum clocks in Britain.

One advertisement placed by Ahasuerus Fromanteel offered pendulum clocks both 'at his house on the Bank-side In Mosses Alley, Southwark, and at the sign of the Mermaid in Lothbury' – Loomes' premises. It appeared in a newspaper on the same day as a report of Cromwell's funeral.

The ensuing rule of Cromwell's son Richard was short-lived and by 1660 the monarchy had been restored, with Charles II looking to avenge his father's death.

Professionally, Loomes was in a prime position to cash in on the latest in clock technology thanks to Fromanteel's forward thinking. Yet the political atmosphere continued to be febrile. For trying to hide escaping Parliamentarians, Thomas Loomes was arrested in November 1661 but released on bail of £1,000 to be of 'loyal and peaceable behaviour'. It was a considerable sum, probably paid partially or in full by his father-in-law.

Fromanteel headed for Amsterdam, where he already had clock-making connections in the shape of Huygens.

Despite his political difficulties, Thomas Loomes worked at the Mermaid until 1664, when he suddenly disappears from the records. Four of his apprentices apparently failed to finish their service.

The following year, the plague was rampant in London, fuelled by hot summer weather. It's likely that Loomes contracted the deadly disease and died, along with as many as 100,000 others in the city, whose bodies were tossed into plague pits, mass burial sites where the victims lay anonymously entangled.

In 1666 the Great Fire of London began in a bakery in Pudding Lane. Fanned by strong winds, it burnt for days between Temple and the Tower of London, with closely packed wooden buildings providing ample fuel for the flames. As it swept through the capital's heart, it erased Loomes' workshop at the Mermaid – and at the same time eradicated the Black Death by killing black rats and the associated fleas.

However, rumours that Loomes was murdered for his political persuasion have also persisted. His wife survived until 1717, with records showing she was a widow by 1668 at least.

Loomes was a master clockmaker for about a dozen years, between 1653 and about 1665, with an estimated 30 clocks that he produced still in evidence today. After Loomes finished the clock that found its way to the Repair Shop, it would have gone to the home of a wealthy customer at a time when most people relied on the chimes of public clocks for timekeeping.

* * *

Almost always, Steve's first job is to clean up working parts. This time the detergent and scrubbing brush were taking off dirt accumulated over centuries. It was slow going, but at the end of the process the cogs were shiny rather than jet black.

With the components under close scrutiny, Steve realised the escapement – that sends power to the pendulum – was a much later replacement. In fact, with the evidence arrayed in front of him, he thought the clock had been re-built as many as 40 times, not always very skilfully.

Step by step, he put each element into action, making small repairs along the way. At one stage he had to carve out a steel wedge and solder it on to correct a misshapen tooth, enabling it to finally work correctly.

At the same time, and following Steve's template, Will was making an oak bracket for the clock to stand on. He made the new wood look rustic with a blend of shellac varnish, made richly dark with a spirit dye.

Steve threaded a chain through the mechanism to attach a weight that runs the clock and its strike. It was a case of experimenting to find the right one and he started with the lightest. Then he attached a replacement pendulum that would keep the clock in time as well as a brass finial on the dome as a 'crowning glory'.

While mystery about clockmaker Loomes has largely been revealed, there remains the question about how Frank's family acquired the timepiece. His grandfather Robert Black, born in 1859, was a one-time owner. Like Frank, he worked in engineering. Robert – and his sons – were molders (aka moulders) in a foundry, preparing a sand mould from a wooden pattern that could be filled with molten iron before being machined to a finish.

It was skilled work and during the industrial revolution, engineers were held in high esteem and relatively well-paid. No one knows if Robert bought the clock or inherited it. However, genealogy has proved that previous generations of his family were involved in agricultural labour. Of course, farming was then associated more with poverty than expendable income, especially given the Highland Clearances of the eighteenth and nineteenth centuries, which saw small-scale farmers evicted by landowners questing for better levels of agricultural production. As a result, numerous displaced Scots moved from the Highlands to the coast, the Lowlands and even to North America and Australia. For Frank, the most critical issue is that the curious and compelling clock is once again in working order.

THE BEDFORD
THEATRE
WINDOWS

During daylight hours it was mute and dark, an imposing landmark standing tall on London's low-rise streets. Yet twice nightly, Camden's Bedford Theatre came alive as it threw open its doors for eager audiences, who filled the auditorium in anticipation of lights, music and sizzling stagecraft.

It wasn't well-heeled city workers that surged up the stairs in time for the shows. The socialites who wanted to see and be seen were about a mile away at London's upmarket theatres, dressed in fur wraps and arriving in horse-drawn carriages. Here at the Bedford it was working-class Londoners who packed into the seats, soaking up the popular tunes or comedy catchphrases of shows that hovered somewhere between operetta and burlesque – and sometimes included both.

On the bill, there was all manner of entertainment. Duets, dancing and dramas; chorus girls and cabaret with a compere; monologues and mimicry; double-entendres and ventriloquists' dummies; slapstick and Shakespeare. Posters advertising packed programmes adorned the neighbourhood, exciting the interest of anyone who had the price of a ticket.

The rafters at the Bedford would be ringing with gales of laughter – or sometimes howls of derision. At the start, audiences weren't necessarily kind, especially when some songs took 30 minutes from start to finish. Performers watched and waited in the wings, anxiously living that cliché about 'the smell of the greasepaint, the roar of the crowds'.

But following a spell of almost boundless enthusiasm for music hall entertainment, the viewing public's affection was lured elsewhere, first by cinema and then by the advent of television.

The Bedford closed its doors for the last time in 1951 and stood derelict for 17 years before finally being pulled down.

One man witnessed the death throes of this grand old lady of the London entertainments scene with a heavy heart. Sean McCarthy was a theatre manager by profession and a theatre aficionado by inclination. Starting in his schooldays, he fostered a life-long love of every facet of theatre history. Not only a performer with a rich voice and a passion for the Bard, he was also a management trainee at Sadler's Wells, a house manager for the Royal Shakespeare Company in Stratford and general manager of the Tyneside Theatre Company.

In addition, he was a fan of Frank Matcham, the peerless and influential theatre and music hall designer, whose blend of intimacy and opulence have rendered his buildings timeless, although only about a third have survived.

In fact, the Bedford was not a Matcham theatre, unlike London's Hackney Empire, Palladium and the Coliseum and Blackpool's Tower Ballroom. It was instead the work of Bertie Crewe, a sometime pupil of Matcham's who signed up to the same bravura style. Thanks to the dazzling Baroque fashion in theatre design at the time, the Bedford served as a celebration of the age. Tastes change though and as the twentieth century wore on, there was no appetite to preserve the work of Matcham or Crewe, although the output of both was prolific. The Bedford was not the only theatre to fall.

Before the mechanical diggers did their worst, Sean retrieved two Victorian stained-glass windows that had once signalled the direction of the boxes and the orchestra to incoming customers. Although the windows with their coloured lights had suffered some damage, he vowed to keep them for posterity and one day bring them back to their former glory.

The windows stayed wrapped in newspaper while Sean's career became further entwined with theatre history. Managing theatres gave

Life-long theatre lover Sean McCarthy

way to writing theatre programmes, then producing a magazine that focussed on past glories under the proscenium arch, called *Theatrephile*. When he died in 2001 aged 54, the windows from the Bedford remained safely stashed away. Now it was his wife Anne's turn to ponder their restoration. Thanks to stained-glass window restorer Matt Nickels, her goal of bringing them back to light-giving life was finally realised at *The Repair Shop*'s 'workshop of dreams'.

When Sean saw the Bedford being pulled down, he more than most knew the chasm that it would leave in theatre history.

Once bare fields, Camden had become a busy London borough, with the arrival first of the Regent's Canal in 1820, then the railways, the twin arteries of industrialisation. Nearby, competing railway companies built three major stations: Euston, King's Cross and finally St Pancras.

In the construction of St Pancras, many of the slums that had accumulated in the area were swept away. However, the neighbourhood remained populous, not only with railway workers but notably gin makers and piano manufacturers, among other trades. Pubs sprang up on street corners but the Bedford Arms Tavern, which had opened in the 1820s, distinguished itself by serving tea as well as ale, making itself a venue suited to female customers as well as men. Then it added a 'song and supper' room, with the audience providing the entertainment, for which they might have been rewarded with a drink.

The concept was so popular that in 1861 the tavern was pulled down to make way for the 'old Bedford', a theatre built at a cost of £5,000. Tickets for its 1,168 seats on three tiers were sixpence in the hall, ninepence in the stalls or a shilling on the balcony and every man was permitted to bring two women with him for free.

As a music hall it was a great success, but the building, with its back-alley entrance, was acknowledged as 'small and inconvenient'. As a consequence, the owners bought four neighbouring houses in order to expand. The lights in the old theatre dimmed in 1898, but this time for just a few months while the 'new' Bedford was built. It finally opened in triumph in 1899 with electric lighting, radiators, lavatories and even a sliding roof to provide ventilation.

A newspaper account from the time gives a glimpse of the treat in store for theatre-goers.

It describes the outside in lavish terms, with a symmetrical, stone-clad grand façade with polished red granite embellishments and decorative columns topped by slate rooves and a copper dome, itself crowned with ironwork and rising about 60 feet above the street.

Now, Camden's customers felt like theatre-goers up west, as they entered through a set of marble steps into a spacious entrance hall with a generous assortment of plaster decorations, a gilded ceiling and a marble mosaic floor.

The style of decoration throughout is Louis Quatorze, with a plentiful introduction of free figure paintings in friezes and panels, the effect of gold and soft tints being singularly harmonious when backed up by the rich ruby tints of the plush curtains and seating.

Just up the road in Camden another music hall theatre was opened the following year, reflecting just how popular the entertainment was at the time. The greatest era of theatre building was from the 1880s to the start of the First World War. Over 1,000 professional theatres were operating in Britain then, some built by syndicates who created chains of touring houses.

The stained-glass windows saved by Sean are one of the few surviving artefacts from the Bedford.

However, thanks to the work of artist Walter Richard Sickert, the interiors of the Bedford, old and new, have been captured on canvas.

The post-impressionist painter – a member of the Camden Town Group, a loose arts affiliation forged before the First World War – was once an apprentice to James Whistler. He only opted for a career as an artist after a short and lacklustre attempt at acting.

Afterwards, Sickert took his cue from artists like Edgar Degas and focussed on subjects in the performing arts. But rather than ballet, Sickert found his inspiration in the music hall.

Thanks to him, performers like Vesta Victoria, Minnie Cunningham and Little Dot Hetherington are forever remembered as they feature in Sickert's paintings. One likeness of Minnie Cunningham is titled with one of her most famous songs: 'It's Not the Hen That Cackles the Most That Lays the Largest Egg'. And recollections of the other performers inevitably provoke a smile. Vesta Victoria, who found fame in America, is still remembered for her most popular ditty, 'Daddy Wouldn't Buy Me a Bow Wow', while Little Dot Hetherington serenaded audiences with her version of 'The Boy I Love Is up in the Gallery'.

Beyond the attractive female stars that Sickert favoured as models, the line-up at the Bedford included comics Charlie Chaplin, Max Miller and Max Wall and singer Gracie Fields. Music-hall sweetheart Marie Lloyd was known to love the venue and chose to spend her 50th birthday there, performing in pantomime.

Ella Shields was a frequent guest, dressed in top hat and tails and singing 'Burlington Bertie from Bow', poking fun at the monied classes while glamorising the 'broken down swell', a familiar caricature of the day.

I'm Burlington Bertie, I rise at ten thirty
And saunter along like a toff
I walk down the Strand with my gloves on my hand
Then I walk down again with them off
I'm all airs and graces, correct easy paces
Without food so long I've forgot where my face is
I'm Bert, Bert, I haven't a shirt
But my people are well off you know
Nearly everyone knows me, from Smith to Lord Rosebr'y
I'm Burlington Bertie from Bow.

Sickert is recalled not only as a talented artist but as a sometime suspect in the Jack the Ripper killings of prostitutes. He certainly displayed a morbid interest in those and other sensational killings of the day, using sombre tones to produce work that recalled linked scenes.

And there's a second slightly macabre link to the Bedford, with one of its singers falling victim to the notorious killer Dr Crippen. Americans Corinne and Hawley Crippen were married when they arrived in the UK in 1897 but both had affairs. After Corinne, whose stage name at the Bedford was Belle Elmore, disappeared in 1910, her torso was discovered beneath the house they shared in Camden Road, Holloway. Although Crippen and his lover, Ethel Le Neve, promptly took a passage to North America, they were recognised by the ship's captain – even while Le Neve was dressed as a boy – who radioed his suspicions to police. Detectives took a faster steam-powered service and were waiting for Crippen when he arrived. After a trial, he was hanged at Pentonville Prison the same year.

Around the time of Elmore's death, theatre programmes had begun to include silent films for the first time, with audiences delighted by the innovation.

When music hall suffered a further decline in popularity in the 1930s, the Bedford was turned over entirely to cinema.

However, after the Second World War live theatre made a return to the stage there, with Donald Wolfit bringing Shakespeare productions to Camden. But neither the Bard nor a spell of staging brand new plays could save the building from its fate.

The closure of theatres causes actress Anne as much pain as it did her late husband. In the past, she has starred in Agatha Christie's long-running show *The Mousetrap* and toured with the hit play *Dancing at Lughnasa*. To her, the theatre feels like home.

The Bedford windows that she brought in arrived in two sizes. The first – that once indicated the route to the boxes – was nearly complete with a central panel and its surround, but the lead holding pieces of stained glass could not be salvaged. Meanwhile, the second was a centre section only. Both included pieces of glass that had been painted with vitreous paints then kiln-fired at about 660°C to fuse the colours to it.

As both central sections were of the same size and design, it seemed fair to assume that the first intact surround could be used as a pattern for the missing parts, so from the outset restorer Matt decided to make the windows a matching pair. It wasn't necessarily a straightforward decision.

He knew Anne would have liked to see the windows as they once were, pristine examples of the Victoriana that she and Sean so admired. Yet making changes to historic windows is something that requires a great deal of consideration, as Matt explained. 'In this case the only alterations were additions, made without changing anything that was original. This is a keystone of an ethical stained glass craftsperson.'

Matt has spent his working life working with stained glass, having been an apprentice to his father Keith who was a master of the craft. Matt is now a conservator at the York Glaziers Trust, the oldest and largest specialist stained-glass conservation studio in Britain, however, he still works closely with his dad on projects, making it feel like the apprenticeship has never really ended.

In the Bedford's windows, Matt identified five different types of glass. Predominantly, it comprised cathedral glass, made when molten glass is fed on to a flat surface and flattened to a uniform thickness through textured rollers. It's a generic term for textured glass commonly found in stained-glass windows in houses. There was also what's known

Anne Marriott and Sean McCarthy on their wedding day

as 'English muffle' and 'reeded' glass, both made in a similar way but each with their own uniquely patterned roller.

There was also red 'flashed' glass, which is mouth-blown and made in two layers, a thicker one, which is clear coated by thinner, coloured one. There were two reasons for this. At the time the colour red was often achieved by adding gold to the glass recipe, so it was an expensive product and this was one way of saving cash. Also, due to the density of this particular colour, if it was made entirely of red glass it would have let very little light through. In Victorian times, flash glass would primarily be red, blue or occasionally green.

Finally, there were four roundels, one in each corner, blown into a ball before being flattened through spinning, creating a tell-tale pinnacle at their heart.

Matt's first step was to take a rubbing of the glasswork that would give him a blueprint of where each piece belonged. Once windows like this have been taken apart, all hope of an accurate recreation vanishes. Glass looks geometric and regimented when it is tucked inside the lead. However, glass is cut by hand and by eye and although some shapes in the design look the same, there may well be fractional differences that aren't instantly apparent. With the blueprint at hand, the next job is to remove the lead holding the glass pieces in place and match each to the drawing. He used two pairs of pliers to pull apart the lead. It's always a challenge. Gripping the tools in the wrong place or with too firm a hand can cause the glass to crack. This time, the original cement used to hold each pane in place was powdery with age.

Next, he sorted through the supplies of salvaged glass that he keeps to match the colours of the intact window. Like Sean, Matt will seize on relics from the Victorian age at demolition sites that would otherwise be destined for the skip. The Victorians had a mastery of pastel tints that's difficult to find replicated today.

In this case, he was alerted to the glass by a building-site manager in Brighton who didn't want to see a set of windows destroyed. 'It is so fortuitous that the site manager saw a value in these particular windows, something which unfortunately doesn't happen often,' Matt explained.

If it wasn't for these particular windows I would not have been able to match the glass tint or the texture so authentically and the finished windows would have lacked an aesthetic appearance. More importantly, a historical link would have been broken. There was such a huge variety of glass made in the Victorian era compared to now, that to have some salvaged glass which matched exactly was fortunate indeed.

All that Matt needed to do was to cut the replacement windows to size, using glass from the intact window as a template.

The glass needs to be held in place by a lead frame. Starting from one corner, Matt began cutting strips to fit, using his lead knife and pinning the metal into place with horseshoe nails. Only when every pane on the piece was in place could he apply solder to fix the joins. For the first time, the window could be lifted from its blueprint. Yet the glass still needed to be properly adhered to the lead with a fresh application of cement. He daubed iron-grey viscous cement across the window that lay before him, obscuring the glass, aiming to get the gloopy mix in the narrow gaps between the glass and the lead. Using a brush, he pushed gently to the window top to encourage the cement in the thin seams. He then turned the window 90 degrees to repeat the process. The window underwent two further turns before it was complete. He credits the method to 'Trev the Lead', a veteran stained-glass craftsman in the trade for more than half a century. 'Historic crafts like this rely so much upon knowledge, tricks of the trade or techniques like this one being passed down,' explained Matt.

It was time to cover the glass again, this time with whiting to absorb moisture from the cement. Both panes looked decidedly frosty as they were left to set. And when the cement had set hard it looked, as Will pointed out, as if a flock of pigeons had settled on it.

The crusty remnants weren't bothering Matt, though. When the whiting had drawn out the moisture, he picked out the window, using a sharp stick to create a clean, crisp line where the lead met the glass. Using a scrubbing brush and a light touch, he removed the rest of the excess cement while Will constructed two frames so the windows could be hung in Anne's home, where they would catch the light.

For Anne, it's a reminder of theatre visits that were a hallmark of the couple's relationship. While others rushed passed them at the interval for drinks and ice cream, they would seek out and admire iconic architecture that contributed to theatre life down the decades.

Said Anne:

The windows were a real connection between Sean and myself.

The fact that we both loved history and had a great sense of the unbroken line connecting theatre – from Grecian masks to the Mysteries to Shakespeare to Garrick, Olivier and onwards – made things like these windows as well as the beautiful ceilings and statuary to be found inside so many theatres an embodiment of that connection.

Before we left after a theatre visit we would take a last glance at the theatre when the auditorium returns to a rather magical, sometimes spooky, state of anticipation. It still feels alive, though no one is sitting in the seats and the sound of everyone leaving gets fainter. At that point, there was a moment to absorb the splendour of our surroundings, without being elbowed or trampled. The joy of the theatre, during opening hours or as it closed, never left us.

A STRONGWOMAN'S DRESS

I n an age where Hollywood stars set the benchmark for beauty, Joan Rhodes had everything going for her. At 5 feet 7 inches tall and with a 22-inch waist she was statuesque, striking and elegant. The term 'blonde bombshell' was coined for her by some – but there was more to Joan than good looks.

She didn't maintain her reputation by casting sultry glances or sexy pouts into a camera lens in the same way as Jayne Mansfield and Marilyn Monroe, who both bore a passing resemblance to her. Instead, she was a strongwoman who carved out a cabaret career by amazing audiences with her physical prowess.

Joan could lift grown men, several of them, at one time. She tore up telephone directories and bent iron bars. When she chose to she could carry a dining table in her teeth. Yet after all these extraordinary exploits, and many similar ones, she left the stage without a hair out of place; there wasn't a chip in her glossy nail varnish nor a broken stiletto heel.

One of the sobriquets that was more applicable then was 'The Mighty Mannequin', which is how she was billed on theatre posters, while she dubbed herself 'an iron girl in a velvet glove'.

Her watchword was glamour and her glitzy costumes were eye-popping. It was one of her hallmark sequin numbers that found its way into the Repair Shop, suffering from signs of wear and tear.

Close friend Triona Holden brought in the emerald-and-silver-fringed basque coupled with a matching split-to-the-waist skirt, having inherited it after Joan's death in 2010. Joan bequeathed a similar one to the Victoria and Albert Museum.

Typically, Joan ripped off the skirt during performances and threw it to one side with a flourish, so it skidded across the stage with a rattle. Inevitably it left a narrow trail of sequins in its wake as the shiny discs popped out of their stitching. Now large bald patches had appeared as the outfit approached its eighth decade.

By any account, Joan's was a life less ordinary that began in 1921 when she was born into a dysfunctional family living in London's East End. Times were tough in the wake of the First World War, with brutalised men returning from the Western Front to find the country in the grip of economic hardship, and a bad situation was made worse by her father's long absences. Eventually, her mother locked her and her siblings in the house and abandoned them.

Neighbours called in the police and Joan was sent to live with an aunt who ran a pub in Smithfields, the home of the capital's meat market at the time. Customers got an early indication of her innate strength when they saw a 12-year-old Joan lift beer barrels from the cellar.

Eventually, the relationship with her aunt broke down and Joan ran away from home with eight pennies in her pocket, living on the streets of London and finding inspiration in a strong man's act staged by a street performer outside the National Gallery. Aged 14, she began busking as well, learning further tricks of the trade.

In 1939 the National Registration has her living in London with the surname Terene and working as a model and gym instructress. She had begun to appear in variety shows and also as an extra in some films. There were a few appearances as a circus act but these were the exceptions, rather than the rule.

A decade later she spotted an advertisement in *The Stage* magazine that started with the words: 'Freaks Wanted'. It was placed by the showman and impresario Pete Collins, who was already marketing acts like The Human Aquarium (a man who swallowed live fish and could regurgitate them in any given order); The Human Gasometer (who swallowed gasoline, then breathed enough fire to cook an omelette);

The Man with the Xylophone Skull (whose forehead was played like a musical instrument); and The Woman with Ten Brains (who could write independent words and sentences at the same time with chalk attached to her fingers and thumbs). There was also Lofty, a Dutchman who stood at 9 feet 3 inches tall and who performed with 'best friend' Seppetoni, a diminutive 3 feet 6.

When she arrived for an interview Collins told her she did not look much like a freak. In response, she tore up the telephone books in his office before carrying him around the room. It assured her a place in one of his travelling shows called 'Would You Believe It?' where she appeared on the same bill as 'the two tallest men in the world', with Atlas and Tiny both measuring more than 9 feet in height; high-wire clowns Reco and May; Spanish juggler Rostando; and Mushie, the lion that ate a steak from a woman's forehead.

In becoming a strongwoman Joan was joining a long-standing tradition that was familiar to audiences at the time. The previous generation of variety hall audiences had been thrilled by the exploits of the Great Sandwina and Vulcana, who were among a clutch of physically endowed women who displayed super-human strength.

The Great Sandwina (also known as Lady Hercules), who died in 1952, lifted her (amply built) husband above her head with one hand and could resist the pull of four horses. As a child Vulcana trained as a weightlifter and performed with her partner, whose stage name was Atlas. Vulcana, born in 1874, began her career performing at fetes in her native Wales before moving to London and the variety circuit.

Both presented themselves in the style of circus performers and their bodies bore significant outward signs of their physical abilities, with bulging biceps and highly defined backs and stomachs. Key to their success was an ability to disrupt the male stereotype of being the strongest of the species.

With an hourglass figure, Joan wasn't muscle-bound and appeared all the more exotic for that. Her stage garb often included a boa, fishnet tights and impossibly high heels.

In a *Sunday Times* interview, she revealed the typical responses she got from men, who were apparently awed and attracted by her immense

Joan bending an iron bar

strength in equal measure. 'The more intelligent men tend to think "she's stronger than I am," and leave it at that. For others, I become instantly not a woman, but someone they're in opposition to and they try to prove something. The obvious thing is to try to get me into a bedroom … and I'm a sitting-room girl!'

In Britain, Joan became a regular at the Empire chain of theatres, which had more than 50 outlets around the country. Her fame even took her to Windsor Castle, where she performed in front of the royal family.

In addition, she travelled to as many as 50 countries, providing her inimitable brand of entertainment telescoped into an act that usually lasted about 15 minutes. She appeared on the same bill as stars like Marlene Dietrich, Fred Astaire and Sammy Davis Jr. In one memorable Christmas show in Iceland, she picked up Bob Hope, one of the world's greatest stars at the time, but dropped him after tumbling backwards, with a broken stiletto thought to be responsible for the fall. Almost immediately she received a telegram from Bing Crosby, Hope's on-screen sparring partner, declaring: 'It should have happened sooner and harder.'

She invited men from the audience to compete against her in a tug-of-war, with her at the centre point keeping both teams of two in their places. There are pictures of South African heavyweight boxer Ewart Potgieter, an eye-widening 7 feet 2 inches in height, standing on her while she is in a crab position – stomach raised high while she supports her body with her backwards leaning arms and legs. On at least one occasion she picked up a baby elephant.

In 1955, a portrait of her by artist Laura Knight was on display at the Royal Academy Summer Exhibition.

Joan calculated that during her 25 years as a strongwoman she had torn up 25,000 telephone books – sometimes into quarters – and bent more than two and a half tonnes of nails.

As the age of variety gave way to television, she found herself on the small screen in a series called *Dick Turpin*, starring Richard O'Sullivan as the highwayman. Her role was as Big Nell. In films, she won bit parts in Blake Edwards' 1976 classic *The Pink Panther Strikes Again*, starring Peter Sellers as an accident-prone French detective, and *The*

Elephant Man, made in 1980 and starring John Hurt as the circus 'freak show' attraction.

There was talk of her heading over to Hollywood to star in *Tarzania*, a female equivalent of the film version of Edgar Rice Burrough's ape-man. But Joan was reluctant to leave London, where she had a much-loved flat in Belsize Park. She also preferred working with live audiences, who could quickly discern that there was no fakery around her act.

In later life, she ran a café in Crouch End, with stars Annie Lennox and Dave Stewart and students from the Mountview theatre school among her regular customers. She also took up art.

One close friend was Quentin Crisp, the controversial writer and raconteur, who was a dozen years her senior. He dyed his hair, wore make-up and paraded around London in flamboyant costumes, displaying considerable personal courage in a society riven with homophobia.

Years afterwards she told journalists:

> Often on a Sunday, he'd come to my home and I'd always make a roast lunch, which he loved. If it was summer we'd sit in the garden and drink gallons of home-made lemonade and in winter he used to sit in front of the fire.
>
> If I won at Scrabble – which wasn't often – he'd say, 'You've achieved greatness today, Miss Rhodes.' He was very kind and thoughtful, always. When he moved to New York, he wrote regularly. We were friends for more than 50 years.

She published excerpts from their 20-year correspondence after his death in 1999, in which he addressed her as 'my dear Miss Rhodes'.

In December 1981, after moving to America, he wrote:

> I live in what is disparagingly called the Lower East Side. My landlord said to me: 'I have put this rubber ring round your front door key to make it instantly recognisable. You may need to use it in a hurry.'
>
> I live in the same street as Hell's Angels but, secretly, I am relying on their unconditional support.

Joan performing in Germany

After an appearance on an American chat show, it became clear Crisp's telephone number was in the directory.

> The calls have thinned out now but still occur occasionally. Isn't it amazing that not one of them was hostile? One asked me for money; one asked me for a job in television; one asked me for an introduction to Mr Letterman and one was embarrassing.
>
> What a contrast with England where never a day went by without someone screaming through the telephone that he would kill me! If I am killed here, it will be for money, which is sacred. In Britain murder is an act of social criticism.

In 2004, Joan was presented with a Lifetime Achievement Award by the British Music Hall Society. Her 2007 memoir *Coming on Strong* featured an introduction by comedian and actor Roy Hudd, another long-time friend. It was, he insisted, 'One of the very best show business autobiographies I have ever read.'

Joan was in her eighties when she met former BBC anchor Triona Holden, who was researching the lives of unusual women.

'She still exuded a pzazz and sparkle,' Triona recalled. 'I see Joan as a feminist icon.'

* * *

Sara Dennis, an ex-farmer and theatre nurse, was in charge of the repair to Joan's dress. It was in capable hands. After a fine-art degree, Sara qualified as an embroidery tutor at the Royal School of Needlework in Hampton Court Palace.

Examining the dress, she saw it was 'battered and bruised' by its stage appearances, but she didn't want to alter its structure. One area of concern was an apparent home repair on the skirt, which could have been hiding a tear. Using curved scissors she snipped away at the stitches to reveal it had merely been folded over and sewn to disguise still more bare patches.

A decorative clasp on the skirt was, she discovered, made from a pair of clip-on earrings. Attaching them more tidily was a swift fix.

With its glossy shine now dimmed by decades of service, this tea-making samovar had been central to a night-time ritual for Nawzad Khurshid in his childhood home in Iraq. Now he wanted to share the same experience with grandchildren in England.

Repair Shop experts teamed up to help as Will Kirk turned a new wooden handle for the samovar chimney while silversmith Brenton West repaired some failing joints so the samovar was once again safe to handle after being heated by hot coals.

Jay lent a hand as ceramics expert Kirsten Ramsay pieced together a stunning bowl that accompanied a young couple hounded out of their historic homeland in the Second World War – only to be smashed years later by a leaden-footed cat.

Delighted by Kirsten's painstaking and almost invisible repair, Penny later discovered the maker of the bowl had fled persecution by the Nazis just as her grandmother had done.

Hefty volumes of newspaper clippings compiled during a doomed love story were falling apart at the seams until bookbinder Christopher Shaw got to work.

When Jenny Lane returned she was delighted to find the restored volumes relating the epic tale of an heroic ancestor were sturdy again while their vintage character remained intact.

During the Second World War Coastal Command was a 'Cinderella' service, overshadowed by other branches of the Royal Air Force. Until he brought a wartime flying jacket into the Repair Shop, John Lofting had little idea about the key role played by grandfather Harry.

After John was gifted the jacket by his father Graham, leather worker Suzie Fletcher, who'd stitched its fraying seams and repaired a gaping hole in the shoulder, was delighted to discover it was a perfect fit.

Jay and conservator Matt Nickels discovered how stained glass from the auditorium of a music hall brought to the Repair Shop by Anne Marriot symbolised a shared bond rooted in an enduring love of theatre.

Expert Matt – whose working life began as an apprentice to his father – used similar Victorian glass recovered from another demolished building to carry out the renovation.

Together with Jay, needlework expert Sara Dennis heard how Triona Holden considered strongwoman and friend Joan Rhodes a feminist icon.

After the meticulous replacement of lost sequins, the outfit that had once clung to Joan's figure as she wowed audiences with amazing physical feats was again in sparkling form.

When he was a boy, David Taylor filled a metal can to fetch the daily water supply for his family as they travelled the country with a fairground attraction.

Metalworker Dom Chinea eased out the can's rusty base and forged a replacement. With help from Brenton West, he made the item rust-free and water-tight once more.

A sewing table with its neat compartments became a platform for the fond childhood memories of Christine Farmer during an era of 'make do and mend'.

When Will Kirk got to work, he opted to save all that remained of the original veneer so the table would retain its character and be familiar to Christine in her child's-eye view.

However, when it came to sewing on sequins to disguise the bald patches on the items, there was nothing quick about the operation.

Sequin is an old Arabic word for 'coin'. Reflective metal discs like the ones that smothered Joan's outfit became popular in the 1920s as a symbol of wealth and extravagance. When this costume was made in the fifties there wasn't the same range of shiny materials that exist today. Sequins were the favourite option for making performers glisten under spotlights.

When the lined basque and skirt were first made, each sequin was sewn on by hand. Now Sara was repeating the process – and the more she looked at the garments, the more bald patches she saw. After removing the lining and tying silk thread to a fine curved needle, her nimble fingers set about a task that she admitted was 'repetitive and time consuming'. However, as she rarely works with sequins, it was a challenge she also relished.

The first problem she and Jay encountered was to find sufficient replacement sequins in the right colour range. When that was established, she had some made of metal while others were plastic, but all looked too shiny to blend in. Sara tried several ways of weathering them, including dipping them in acetone and putting them through a washing machine. In the end, she discovered rubbing them with a fine sandpaper was the only way to make them look suitably 'distressed'.

On close inspection of the garment, she found evidence of a few more rushed repairs, done 'on the hoof', probably within hours of the stage curtain being lifted. These were made good.

But disaster struck when Sara realised the original sequins had been attached by a technique called tambour. This entailed a fine, sharp hook punched through a fabric to catch the sequin, creating a chain-like stitch. When a thread came loose, a whole row of sequins came away, considerably multiplying the number of sequins that needed to be sewn.

There were also cracked sequins, which were either more firmly attached with a stitch or replaced. Before the job was done, about 500 new sequins had been individually fastened to the outfit and it took an estimated 50 hours to accomplish the repair. Even then, there were still small patches with exposed fabric. But Sara was mindful to leave some evidence of the outfit's advanced age and rich past. No one, least of all Triona, wanted it to look as new. When Sara called a halt to her repair, the result was stunning.

The final focus for attention was on the crotch of the basque, where Sara stabilised the frayed seam with pins and used ordinary sewing thread in a ladder stitch so the mending work was invisible. She then replaced the lining, using a slip stitch.

After she saw the repaired outfit, Triona felt Joan herself had been brought back to life because it lit up the room, just as she once did.

The pair were friends and confidantes despite a 40-year age gap. Following their first meeting, Triona became a regular visitor, finding Joan, who lived alone, charming and compelling company. She believes Joan's outlandish strength was fuelled by an anger that stemmed from her fractured childhood.

An experienced journalist and author, Triona covered wars, famine and other catastrophes but left the BBC after developing lupus, an auto-immune disease for which there is no cure. Joan encouraged Triona as she changed her career from journalism to art – as Joan herself had made a similar journey from variety performance into painting.

In return, Triona supported Joan through her final battle with breast cancer and was with her when she died. Since then the dress resided on a mannequin in Triona's bedroom, to where it will return.

'Joan was like a mother to me, she encouraged me to become an artist. I keep [the costume] with me as a constant reminder that Joan believed in me and when I look at it, I am driven to make her proud.'

Triona is now writing Joan's life story as a tribute. 'This costume represents the epitome of Joan. She was a remarkable woman and deserves to be remembered for her achievements. The costume sparkles just as she did right up to the day she died.'

A FAIRGROUND
WATER CAN

Sometimes the damp, dark depths of a garden shed can yield unexpected treasures. So it was for David Taylor, who uncovered an intriguing everyday item from his childhood at risk of being consigned to the scrapheap.

When the forgotten metal carrier was dragged into the daylight, it rekindled memories of how he and his younger brother once used to collect water for his fairground family's daily needs.

With it now dented and with rust devouring the bottom, David hoped metalworker Dom Chinea would transform it into a precious memento of an extraordinary life.

Although David called it a water can, it wasn't something that belonged in the veg patch. It better resembled a milk churn with a handle and a spout, one of three used by the family who lived all year round in accommodation that didn't have running water.

In its prime, it was painted sky blue to match a family caravan and was distinguished by a shiny brass name plate bearing his mother's name, Mrs J. Taylor, which David insists was the travelling community's domestic equivalent to 'a bit of bling'. It was in his mother's shed that the prized item had lay hidden.

During the fifties and early sixties, he and his brother Stephen perched the trio of containers on a boarded Silver Cross pram frame before they set off to find the nearest tap. When the family were settled in their winter quarters in Chertsey, Surrey, that was at the back of a local corner shop. At sites they visited across southern Britain in the summer months, the standpipe they needed could be anywhere in the locality. The water they brought back was for drinking, washing and washing-up.

David was born into a long-established fairground family, with dad William the owner of a shooting gallery in which customers used rifles that fired real bullets. With the sideshow on the move between Easter and September, it was visited at various locations by police who would examine William's licence to operate the weapons. However, the officers weren't unduly concerned about any other aspects of public safety! Afterwards, the shooting gallery was open to customers who were offered five shots for a shilling. Typically, it was teenagers and Teddy Boys who would try their luck but anyone tall enough to see above the front parapet was welcome to take a chance.

On one occasion, a drunk who took his chances with David's mum Jean found himself on the business end of a rifle, with her taking aim and firing at his foot.

Usually, it was ducks, bottles and targets in the crosshairs, as they were dragged mechanically across the back of the stall. Targets could be wound into the front of the stall on a length of string to check the accuracy of the shooter. For the lucky winners, there was what fairground people knew as 'swag', including stuffed toys and glassware that were bought from hawkers out of giant tea chests. Grandfather Bill ran a hoopla stall with similar gifts on offer.

Although William was only semi-literate, he and his father were practical men who could turn their hands to anything. Bill once built a steam engine for a fairground owner from scratch. And together he and William converted a bus built by the Guildford company Dennis into a mobile family home. Windows were blocked out, there were two bedrooms – one with bunk beds – and there were even a fireplace and a cooking range. The bus towed the shooting range and sometimes a second load behind that as well. Prior to the age of motorways, the speeds the convoy achieved on narrow roads were awesomely slow. It was to this novelty vehicle that David would be delivering the water cans.

Joining the family in the summer were men called 'chaps', young labourers who helped to put up and take down the stall in its various locations, particularly the hefty one-inch-thick metal plates that lined the back of the sideshow to stop poorly aimed bullets mid-flight. The 'chaps' were often ex-servicemen who struggled to find work after the Second World War. During the day they shared meals with the family, while at night they slept under the vehicle.

Although David and his siblings didn't attend school during the summer months, there was still an education of sorts. All fairground children learned mental maths quickly when they manned various stalls on behalf of their families. While they weren't coached in English like other children their age, they learned elements of the Romany language that had been handed down for generations and also mastered 'backslang', the ability to say words backwards as part of regular conversation so customers at fairground kiosks wouldn't understand what they were saying. His uncle, Walter, was one of the most talented painters in the business, sought after to decorate rides in the boldest, brightest designs that evolved with popular culture, so lessons in art were scaled up to the sides of swing boats or the bodywork of dodgem cars.

Then there was what most might recognise as a broader education in life. One neighbour at a fairground was a man with a head that was shaved except for a plait at the back. During nightly shows, David saw him lie on a bed of nails and have concrete blocks piled on his chest or throw knives around the silhouette of the woman who later became his wife. As children, David and his brother were beckoned into the man's trailer to watch slack-jawed as he put two barbecue skewers through his cheeks, by way of a rehearsal.

There was a boxing ring where fighters invited all-comers to try their luck. Anyone who could put the fighter on the canvas was in line for a prize – although few did. British boxing champion Freddie Mills was a fairground-booth fighter before the Second World War and died by a bullet from a fairground rifle.

David's family rented pitches from major fairground owners with names that are familiar throughout the industry: Roses, Guests and Botton & Traylens.

Eventually, William had the shooting gallery made into a permanent fixture on the back of a lorry and bought a caravan. Now the lorry towed the caravan – although there was still no running water.

While David and his siblings were probably the envy of their winter classmates, there were disadvantages to being seasonally itinerant. There was, for example, plenty of abuse from people who didn't care for their lifestyle choices and failed to appreciate long-standing showman culture. As a consequence, they found themselves barred from pubs and shops.

There was also an element of fierce tribalism. For example, fairground folk like the Taylors who came from South London were hostile to rivals in Hampshire and fists were likely to fly if one encroached on the territory of the other.

With both his parents coming from showman families, David has discovered a wealth of anecdotes about his ancestors. Jeremiah Taylor

The Taylor family at the fairground

was one of them, who died after a bare-knuckle fight on Wimbledon Common in 1831, aged 46. He wasn't killed by a punch but tripped on his flapping sock and hit his head, dying 12 hours later. His bereaved wife Sarah later asked for leniency to be shown to opponent William Faulkner because it was, she said, a fair fight.

Also in his family tree is Frank Wilson, better known as 'Lorenzo' the lion tamer. It wasn't always plain sailing as one report from the *Darwen News* in 1891 reveals. As a lion called Wallace turned nasty, Lorenzo nearly had his legs pulled from under him by the big cat.

> The greatest terror spread amongst the spectators but Lorenzo – Frank had elected a few years earlier to assume a rather more charismatic name – acted with great coolness and courage. He remained standing, by a desperate effort, and then commenced to fight with the beast, eventually making it relax its hold.

Despite his injuries, Lorenzo elected to finish the performance and left the ring to resounding applause.

Nor was that terrifying incident his only brush with death. A few months earlier he had been working with six wolves when one jumped on top of him, snarling and biting. On another occasion, he was bitten by a bear. Frank had married into the Sedgwick family, who owned a menagerie, a popular Victorian and Edwardian attraction that towed exotic animals kept in wagons around the country to stage shows in remote towns. (David's mother Jean was also a Sedgwick.) In 1911, Frank bought a carousel – or galloper – but died months later, not from a lion attack but in his bed after contracting a bad cold.

David's great-grandfather also operated cinema-graphic shows to a curious audience, often captured in action by aspiring film-makers beforehand with the footage broadcast before the main picture. It was marketed as a 'bioscope show'.

The age of steam brought new rides to the fairground in the nineteenth century, including steam yachts and scenic railways. Electric rides were a twentieth-century phenomena, with the dodgems arriving in 1928 and the waltzer five years later. Each new ride was more challenging than the last. But life was changing, with traditional fairs rooted in rural diaries since medieval times losing momentum and other attractions, including holidays abroad, gaining traction. With safety concerns on the rise, static fairgrounds became a popular option.

When David was in his teens, his father decided to give up life on the road. With one wary eye on the success of television and concern for the education of David and Stephen's younger siblings, Kim and Stewart, he chose life as a 'flattie', fairground language for anyone in the settled population. William got a job as a driver working for Courage Breweries, based in Staines, Middlesex, a company that eventually provided employment for many of the Taylor family. David himself worked there, training to be a Master of Wine until the site was shut down in the seventies. He went on to establish a career with British Airways in customer relations.

* * *

For Dom, the process was straightforward but not without its challenges for all that. The rusted can bottom had to be replaced, but Dom wanted to lever it out in one piece so he could use it as a template for a replacement. It seemed like the chances of getting it out whole were unlikely until he noticed its seams had been soldered. As a result, he heated them up and extracted the nibbled circle in one piece.

With the bottom out and the plaque and handle removed, Dom could knock out some of the major dents in the body of the can using a dolly hammer.

Using the original for accurate sizing, Dom made a steel circle. He wanted the replacement base to be a replica of the original, down to the outside edge that was turned up to create the mounting flange and an indented circle in the centre, there to add strength.

To recreate it he used a bead roller, a modern electrical version of a traditional machine. It meant feeding the sheet metal in through two wheels, which are clamped together under pressure to manipulate the sheet steel as desired. A versatile machine, it's capable of hundreds of different profiles of wheels, for specific jobs.

Dom is something of an expert at TIG welding. The initials stand for tungsten inert gas and it's a commonly used welding technique when it comes to fixing steel into place. It's the preferred way of welding sheet steel when you can fuse two pieces together without adding extra material, leaving a much stronger and cleaner join. But on this occasion, it wasn't suitable because the temperatures involved would soar during the process and risked melting the solder holding the rest of the can together. Also, the high heat could have distorted the thin body of the can.

So he asked Brenton, the acknowledged expert at soldering in the barn, to help. Following the silversmith's advice, Dom brushed the exposed seams with flux to stop the metal oxidising and inserted the steel ring, which was then gripped into place by tools as Brenton worked his way around with a hand-held solder gun. In fact, it took longer to undertake the cleaning process than to do the soldering. However, it was critical that the surfaces were clean so that the solder would stick. If the solder failed, there was the risk of a leaving a pinprick hole.

To test their workmanship, they poured water into the container – to find with some relief that there were no leaks. Jay then sent the can away to be galvanised, which means applying protective zinc to protect the metal from rust. As the process involves dipping articles into a bath of molten zinc, it's carried out away from *The Repair Shop* site.

Although he initially feared the spout would have to be removed, Dom discovered a small repair to the inside flange was sufficient.

Using flakes of the original paint that he'd saved, Dom made a colour-match and spray-painted the body of the can a familiar sky blue.

David told Dom how the can had been painted in a classic 'showman style' and explained how 'Gypsies and showmen had distinctive artworks. Gypsies used flowers and we used pinstripes'.

With William's long-standing allegiance to Aston Villa football club in mind, Dom painted the pinstripes around the can in claret.

When he was reunited with the can, David was momentarily overcome. An object once so familiar, which represented a way of life now unknown to him, was once again in his hands, looking like new. The sight of his mother's name on the glittering plate was particularly affecting.

'It has been transformed from a wreck to a work of art,' he told Dom – and would now serve as a reminder of a childhood that he acknowledged as the best time of his life. 'I absolutely loved travelling the country with my best friends. Living in a fairground is a paradise for any kid.'

A BUTTER
CHURN

When the Second World War erupted, it changed the destiny of thousands of people, 18-year-old Laetitia Hibbert among them.

Before the war, she was a carefree debutante whose primary concerns were clothes and cocktail parties. Afterwards, she was mostly seen in rolled-up sleeves and wellies, ready to milk a cow or round up stragglers from a flock of sheep. A broken-down butter churn that found its way to the Repair Shop was a symbol of her transition from landed gentry to Women's Land Army (WLA).

Hostilities began when Laetitia was just 18 years old. The only daughter of a retired army officer, she was already listed as having private means. But life at her family home, Hennor House, in Leominster, Herefordshire, was turned upside down when it was requisitioned for the recuperation of injured soldiers. At once she volunteered to nurse them, although she found she still had time on her hands when she wasn't needed in the wards.

Determined to do her bit towards the war effort, Laetitia joined the WLA, a new initiative started just prior to the outbreak of war to bring young, single women into food production on Britain's farms. For WLA director Lady Gertrude Denman, there was no doubt the women coming into its ranks were as heroic as everyone else in uniform.

'The land army fights in the fields,' she declared. 'It is in the fields of Britain that the most critical battle of the present war may well be fought and won.'

This battle was because the perilous threat of submarine warfare loomed large. At the time, Britain imported 70 per cent of its food and that all arrived by ship. There was grain from North America – produced much more cheaply on the prairies than wheat in Britain – and fruit, cheese and butter from the colonies spread across the globe. As a consequence, Britain had the largest merchant navy in the world – amounting to one-third of all non-military shipping in existence – but its vessels were no more than sitting ducks to U-boats that patrolled the Atlantic.

And if German U-boats blockaded British ports – preventing merchant ships laden with food supplies from getting through – there was a serious risk of starvation for those on the home front.

To counter it, conscientious objectors, refugees, the unemployed and even schoolchildren were directed to farms to lend a hand, but the numbers weren't nearly enough to avert any impending crisis. Then the Government earmarked women for agriculture to replace men that had joined the forces. (Even then, in September 1940 the Cabinet agreed that soldiers should help bring the harvest in, for the second year running, in return for free beer from the farmer.) Beyond that, women were also expected to increase productivity. Soon they discovered stepping up food production was a monumental task without end.

There was a uniform that volunteers like Laetitia wore: cream shirts, green jumpers, corduroy breeches and a three-quarter length brown overall with deep pockets and four buttons down the front.

Almost immediately, women dressed like this appeared in the fields, shouldering all kinds of work.

Much later, one woman who went to Leominster with the WLA from Leeds recalled the jobs that confronted her and her colleagues.

Our jobs were many and varied. Hoeing, (hoe-so boring) thistle bodging, stone picking, hay making, stacking corn, building hay and wheat ricks, loading the carts and leading the horses for the ploughing. Spud planting and picking was a hated job, especially in the rain, struggling to pull our feet out of that mud, sometimes leaving our wellies behind, dragging our buckets behind and longing to be rained off.

Laetitia Hibbert-Foy

There was also muck-spreading, beet pulling, hedging, ditching, hop-picking and shaking the apples out of trees. One group became rat-catchers as there were an estimated 50 million rodents in Britain at the time, poised to eat their way into valuable crops. Using poison as bait, the women turned into merciless killers, with each accounting for as many as 6,000 rats a year.

None of the women were richly rewarded. At first, the minimum pay was 28 shillings for a 48-hour week, with half deducted for board and lodgings. Men were paid 10 shillings more for doing the same jobs.

By the autumn of 1941, there were 20,000 women in the WLA but it wasn't enough. Conscription for women was introduced in December that year alongside a pay rise and overtime (at no more than 11 1/2d per hour). Already the WLA had proved they were making a difference with output over three years increased by an impressive two-thirds.

Although recruitment was halted in 1943 as women were steered to aircraft factories, the numbers rose to 80,000 the following year after they were being taken on again. A third were estimated to be city-dwellers. A quarter did dairy work.

A wartime book that acted as a recruiting sergeant was frank with would-be land girls.

It's hard work, make no mistake about that; you do a man's job which is why you must be physically fit when you are enrolled. Town girls whose civilian jobs have been sedentary may feel very tired for the first week or two but it's a healthy tiredness that soon passes and I've seen thousands of such girls looking not only fitter and happier but infinitely more attractive after a week or two in the Service.

In 1942, the fitness of some was put to the test with the creation of the Timber Corps, established by the Ministry of Supply. Six thousand 'lumber Jills' began felling and stacking tree trunks as they became responsible for providing pit props and telegraph poles.

Experiences of hostile farmers providing Spartan accommodation and next-to-no food, which were infamous at the start of the conflict, gave way to hostels in which there was a warm camaraderie.

Although German submarines were initially effective, the British organised merchant ships into convoys, which were assisted by the Americans even before the US entered the war and ultimately used information gleaned by the code-breakers at Bletchley Park to avoid predator U-boats. The Battle of the Atlantic was finally won, albeit at a cost of some 30,000 merchant seamen drawn from across the empire, who perished on 4,700 ships bearing a British flag that were dispatched to the ocean floor by enemy action.

By working in the fields, the WLA played its part in the Battle of the Atlantic, reducing the burden on the merchant navy and thus helping to keep the nation – and its livestock – fed. There were other key measures that played into the same theme, like the 'dig for victory' campaign that encouraged householders to turn their gardens into an allotment and keep backyard poultry. Then there was rationing, which limited access to specified groceries.

At first, the imposition of ration books was portrayed as a government infringement of civil liberties by an outraged national media. Rationing finally came into effect in January 1940, with everyone receiving a book that would limit the amount they could buy of items including butter, sugar, cheese and meat. Customers had to register with the shop where their ration books would be used so there was no question of shopping around. Also, everything still had to be paid for and thus was subject to inflation. Crucially, the rationing system implied everyone from the royal family downwards would be treated the same, that people would get their fair share. In reality, food was more plentiful in rural areas – where there was access to items like butter churns – than it was in towns, while some people still had enough spare cash to buy foodstuffs from the busy black market that quickly evolved. Rations changed as the war progressed and continued after the conflict ended.

The WLA also continued after the war, being run by a government still struggling to harvest sufficient food for the nation. 'One more

Martin and Laetitia Foy in 1948

furrow' was the official rallying cry. At the end of hostilities, there was an international food shortage, with a worldwide deficit of 1,800,000 tonnes of meat predicted that year. In 1947, some 54,000 women were still working on the land, often alongside prisoners of war. The last WLA workers were demobbed in 1950.

Despite the labours of the women and their acknowledged triumph in the fields, the WLA earned a reputation as the Cinderella service for the lack of official recognition, with Lady Denman resigning over the government's decision to exclude its ranks from any post-war financial benefits.

There's no record of Laetitia's experiences, although she may even have worked in the kitchen garden attached to her fifteenth-century home, as the generously proportioned vegetable patches tucked up in the walled gardens of large estates were also on the jobs list for the WLA. For her, it would have been a slightly different experience than most. She knew Queen Elizabeth – who became patron of the WLA in July 1941 – as a personal friend. In 1941 she married Martin Foy, a former Essex regiment officer who started intelligence work.

The couple started farming, first in Leominster and later in Kent, at a time when food production was changing beyond recognition.

Firstly, rewards for farming had increased considerably during the war. When it started, the price for one hundredweight (cwt) of wheat was 5 shillings, but six years later that had risen to 14 shillings and 5d. It was a similar story for oats, while the price of barley had risen threefold. Subsidies by the Ministry of Agriculture were now a factor but other advances also played into the changing face of farming.

In 1940 there were six times as many horses as tractors working the land. Moreover, some of the tractors were still static and steam-powered. All that was about to change, with tractors powered by a combustion engine becoming ubiquitous. After the war, farmers responded to price guarantees given by the government with investment in machinery, stock, farm buildings and pesticides, all directed at raising production levels.

One effect was to substantially bring down the price and increase the availability of chickens and turkeys, which had previously been considered luxury meats. But the flip side of the same coin meant the cost to consumers for all food fell, hitting farmers' incomes.

In 1962, Rachel Carson published *Silent Spring*, outlining the environmental harm that indiscriminate use of powerful chemicals was wreaking on the countryside.

So farming life wasn't always easy after the war, as Laetitia and husband Martin discovered. While keeping a wary eye on the latest advances in farming technology, Laetitia didn't forget the lessons she had learnt during the privations of war and continued to make butter in a churn taken from Hennor House.

To improve the taste, she kept two Jersey cows named Bluebell and Arabella to provide rich milk that produced the tastiest butter.

One of the life lessons she taught granddaughter Carolyn was how to milk the cows and make butter in the churn. Laetitia poured the creamy top of freshly drawn milk into the churn's barrel, which perched on a wooden stand so it could rotate. As a girl, Carolyn turned the chunky metal handle that made the barrel spin. The butter-making process could take anything from 20 minutes to 2 hours. At first, there was a

sloshing sound as liquid hit the sides of the barrel, but that diminished as the fat in the creamy milk began to coagulate. When the spinning was finished, the butter-maker used hands to agitate it some more until it looked something like scrambled eggs. Using paddles, Laetitia then knocked the butter into shape and the pats were wrapped in greaseproof paper, which were tied up with string. Left to her own devices, Carolyn used to carve pictures in the butter before they were wrapped.

Carolyn was cared for by Laetitia and Martin while her mother, model Fiona Foy, worked in London and America. With limitless amounts of fresh air and the warmth of a loving family, Carolyn knew an idyllic childhood.

Her life as an adult was less blessed. She had to leave her job at a software giant after being diagnosed with breast cancer, which prompted a lifestyle change that took her back to the same rural tranquillity she'd known in childhood. In the Peak District there were limestone sculptures, lichen-covered crags and smooth rivers scything through green gorges. Almost by accident, Carolyn started an animal sanctuary, caring for alpacas, sheep, goats, indeed any animal in need. For many years, she was a single mum of three children with a business to run.

When times have been eye-wateringly tough – and even when they haven't been – she has clung to the belief that she was living the life she was meant to live. The butter churn, representative of her grandmother's transition from aristocrat to being hands-on agriculturally adept, had lived in the back of a barn since Laetitia's death in 2001. Now Carolyn felt the time was right to restore it and celebrate a link to the past.

When she brought it to the Repair Shop, the churn's wood was dry and cracked, it was missing a metal hoop and the metalwork clasps and handles were so rusty it was almost impossible to discern the maker's proud boast of it being a 'champion churn'.

After stripping the metalwork off the barrel, Dom wanted to see if it would hold water. But when he poured hot water inside, it immediately started seeping out of the joints as the wood had dried out during its years of storage. When wood dries like this, it shrinks, and that's what had caused the leaky gaps and allowed the hoop to fall off. His first job was to soak the barrel in hot water overnight to rehydrate the wood.

The next day, master cooper Alistair arrived, an expert at making casks from steamed wood bound by metal hoops. It's a skill that's been around since Roman times but is rarely used in modern storage.

Even now, Alistair doesn't use the swift blade of a power-driven grinder to cut the necessary metal bands but prefers a chisel, lined up on the chalk mark that indicates the correct length, which is struck by a hefty hammer. Coopers' hammers come in three sizes, with apprentices using the smallest at 3½lb. Alistair uses the biggest – a 5½lb version. Rivets are driven into place the same way before the newly forged hoop is knocked into place over the head of the barrel. Even Dom – no slouch when it comes to wielding hefty tools – found the hammer seriously heavy.

Meanwhile, all the metalwork from the churn has been blasted back to bare metal, ready for a coat of a hard-wearing satin black paint. Before the process, Dom had spotted the lettering on the metalwork was originally in yellow. He managed to colour-match one of the last remaining flakes and then painstakingly highlighted them again. The brass clasps that hold milk inside while it is being churned were once again gleaming.

For Carolyn it was an overwhelming experience, reviving childhood memories of a simpler time.

A MINER'S
LAMP

The safety lamp, dubbed the most vital invention in the history of mining, has changed little in design since it was conceived by inventor Sir Humphrey Davy back in 1815.

The idea behind it is simple enough. It's a rudimentary lantern with its flame encased in a wire gauze chimney. Holes in the gauze let the light out but stop firedamp – the name for dangerous underground gases, including methane – from being ignited. Davy had discovered that a small grade mesh can stop a flame in its tracks.

After use of the safety lamp became widespread, the number of underground explosions fell, slashing the list of fatalities, and pitmen could venture deeper than ever before, increasing productivity.

But mining remained a perilous job. Explosions still happened as for some time men insisted on taking candles into the pits, preferring the sharper light thrown by a naked flame, while other hazards, such as floods and roof falls, continued to occur.

More than a century later, the safety lamp was still the first thing that miners reached for before plunging beneath the ground for a day's toil. The science remained the same but its case was now stouter.

When Hubert John took his safety lamp to light the day's labours at Hook Colliery in Pembrokeshire, Wales, on one shift in 1930, he had no reason to imagine it would not only light his path but save his life. It wasn't the threat of explosion that was stalking the mine shafts that day but that of a collapsing roof.

With Hubert squeezed into one of the narrow mine tunnels when it happened, he was at risk of being crushed. But the lamp acted like a wedge and supported the pit prop bearing down on him until rescuers arrived.

His granddaughter Rita Evans brought the lamp into the Repair Shop in the hope that she could light it again in memory of Hubert's extraordinary life.

In the early decades of the twentieth century, there was a trio of notoriously risky occupations: railways, mining and the army. Hubert had his fair share of all three.

Born in Rosemarket, Pembrokeshire, in 1898 he started his working life as an engine cleaner in Llanelli station, with employers the Great Western Railway Company paying him a miserly two shillings and four-pence a day.

At the time, the public was concerned about the menace of rail crashes, but, in fact, the railway was far more hazardous for its workers, with men being hit by engines, crushed at the buffers, falling from wagons, bashed by hydraulic lifting gear and scalded by water from boilers. Nearly 4,000 deaths or serious injuries were recorded between the start of 1911 and the middle of 1915 – the time Hubert worked at the railway. Although by now there were orphanages run by the railway companies and GWR ran an insurance scheme for its workers, the loss of a breadwinner usually sentenced families to lives of poverty. Bad feeling against the GWR and the government was rumbling on after two men were shot in Llanelli in 1911 during a railway strike.

For many men, army life held attractions, not least for an enhanced pay packet, even when there were a troubling number of casualties in the First World War. About 100,000 railwaymen nationwide answered the call to the colours, with approximately one fifth failing to return. Once in uniform, many former railwaymen found themselves working on the extensive system of locomotives and tracks behind the trenches.

However, Hubert's army records were lost in 1940, along with countless thousands of others, when Luftwaffe bombs rained down on London. All that's left is a slip of paper that shows he served in the

Hubert John in his army uniform

Liverpool Regiment, then the Labour Corps, probably being transferred there after an injury.

However, oral tradition is strong in Wales even now and Hubert told his family about experiences in the conflict – in which more than 700,000 British soldiers died – around a hushed dinner table or by a flame-licked hearth.

At his knee, they learned about rat-infested trenches and uniforms riddled with lice, the smell that lingers after a gas attack and the pounding of a bombardment before the shredding blast of a whistle, sending men 'over the top'. Men suffered from searing coughs and gnawing skin conditions as they contended with loneliness, fear and mental exhaustion.

Inevitably, as the conflict drew to an end, men relished the opportunity to return home. But for Hubert, the longed-for reunion with family and friends was delayed as he was ordered directly to Ireland, where a simmering conflict was accelerating into a full-blown one.

Despite being promised Home Rule, Ireland's most ardent Republicans had struck a blow against Britain in 1916 with the Easter Rising. Immediately, troops were shipped from Liverpool to restore order and the battle, centred on Dublin's General Post Office, lasted for six days. Given the deaths of more than 300 civilians, the rebels were initially reviled by the public. But nationalism was stirred even in its mildest advocates by the brutal response of the British government, which ordered the execution of 15 ringleaders.

The dispute festered, something of a sideshow while the First World War was in progress. Although it was still part of the British Empire, elections in 1918 had revealed a huge majority in favour of independence and Sinn Fein, the party that won the most seats, declared itself the government.

As a consequence, the IRA began waging a guerrilla campaign, with the police force having been declared a legitimate target. Irish veterans returning from the front found that the political landscape had changed and, as marked men for their service to the empire, they had to pick sides.

In one corner there was the Royal Irish Constabulary, soon to incorporate the infamous Black and Tans, supported by the British Army. In the other, the Irish Republican Army.

It's not known precisely where Hubert fitted into this often-forgotten war taking place on the domestic front. He might have been part of the British Army platoons dispatched to keep the peace during the election. If he didn't serve in the reviled Black and Tans recruited from around the UK, men just like him did. Whatever he experienced there, his time in Ireland stayed with him for decades afterwards.

Initially, the British Government saw it as a military problem and helped out. However, the RIC was left sorely in need of new recruits after Westminster politicians then judged the savage clash to be solely a policing matter. Advertisements started to appear offering jobs for a wage of ten shillings a day, with free living quarters and one month's leave on full pay in every twelve, with a railway pass home.

The poster outlined the calibre of men being sought: 'If you have the physique, if you have a good character and especially if you are an ex-serviceman …'

The men that flocked to its ranks became known as the Black and Tans, a name inextricably linked to this turbulent spell in Irish history. More militia than police force, some of the men in its ranks were responsible for violence against civilians and extra-judicial killings as the island of Ireland became a battleground.

The men earned the name of Black and Tans for their clothing. When promises of a free uniform came to nothing, they found themselves resorting to one dark-coloured item issued from the RIC matched with something khaki from their British army days. Another name they are remembered by is 'the ten bob a day soldiers', referencing their generous rate of pay.

One-third of the force were Londoners and a further third came from Glasgow and Liverpool, while one-fifth of the men were recruited in Ireland itself. Fewer than five per cent hailed from Wales. Typically, the men were mid-twenties, low-skilled, Protestant ex-soldiers.

A cycle of police assassinations followed by brutal reprisals began, with both sides guilty of appalling abuses. Before the Anglo-Irish Treaty was signed in 1921, 2,000 people had died – 750 of them civilians and 400 policemen.

In Catholic Ireland, the Black and Tans were almost universally loathed, failed to curtail hostilities and did much to rally support for the Irish cause. Violet Asquith, a Liberal activist and daughter of the former prime minister Herbert, was sensitive to their plight.

In an article published in May 1921, she wrote: 'We have to feel sorry for the Black and Tans ... losing their souls in carrying out duties which no Englishman should have been asked to perform.'

For Ireland, there followed a year-long civil war after the establishment of the Irish Free State in 1922. As the schism was shaping up, men like Hubert were horrified by what they saw and experienced and longed to escape.

While it's not clear what Hubert did in Ireland, it's certain that he hated being there. He spoke in ominous terms about it to his family, maintaining: 'It was a war like no other.' As a committed Christian, Hubert would have been challenged by unfolding events. Mining, with its overarching daily threats, now seemed far preferable to being in neighbourhoods quivering with brooding antagonism.

He returned home to Wales, where as many as one in ten people were employed in the coal industry. At the time, coal remained the foundation of civilisation, as journalist George Orwell pointed out in 1937. 'All of us really owe the comparative decency of our lives to poor drudges underground, blackened to the eyes, with their throats full of coal dust, driving their shovels forward with arms and belly muscles of steel.'

Hubert became a hewer, armed with pick and shovel at the coal face, at a time when mechanisation was only slowly making its way into British mines. His primary qualification for the job was stamina. The Hook Colliery in Pembrokeshire, where he worked, had been mined for centuries as it burrowed into seams bearing top-quality anthracite. Commanding high prices at home and abroad, each nugget of the fuel was dubbed a black diamond.

Life was hard for miners everywhere, whose first job when they arrived at work was to put a numbered token around their necks so they could be identified in the event of a disaster that rendered their bodies beyond recognition.

In 1913, 440 miners died in Senghenydd Colliery in Glamorgan following an explosion. Still, men in Welsh mines also died in twos and threes in numerous accidents that didn't garner public attention in the same way. The number of incidents that claimed a few lives rather than many was uncomfortably high and there was, as mining historian John Benson put it, 'the steady drip, drip of death' in the pits. Illness as well as injuries plagued miners, who commonly suffered from health problems like bursitis, also known as beat knee; pneumoconiosis, with symptoms of black spittle and shortness of breath; rheumatism; and sore eyes caused by coal dust and poor light.

Miners could be sometimes distinguished by a characteristic crouch, the position they adopted underground for hours at a time while they chipped away at the coal face. In his essay about mining, Orwell was struck by the bodily contortions required of miners. 'You not only have to bend double, you have also got to keep your head up all the while so as to see the beams and girders and dodge them when they come. You have, therefore, a constant crick in the neck but this is nothing to the pain in your knees and thighs. After half a mile it becomes (I am not exaggerating) an unbearable agony.'

The enforced stoop caused muscular and digestion issues, which were sometimes relieved on the surface by adopting the same rolled-up stance. None of them ate a fried breakfast before work for fear of inducing indigestion. The packed lunch they took down with them would be plain, like bread and jam, for the same reason. Men of the pits were known by the 'buttons' down their back, scabs from sores caused as their spine scraped against the low ceilings.

All pits in Pembroke, being so close to the sea, were prone to sudden flooding. In 1844, 40 men and boys were drowned after water rushed in to fill a cavern in one of the pits there. Two miners were killed at Hook itself in 1916 in the same way. When water penetrated the chambers underground, subsidence became much more likely.

In the mine, safety lamps were like a barometer. When the flame dipped, it indicated oxygen levels were low, and when it flared, there was probably toxic gas in the environment.

But there was no prior indication when a pit would flood – usually when a wall being hacked to relieve it of coal penetrated a submerged chamber – or when a roof might collapse.

Hubert left no account of what happened that day in the mine and no reports of the incident seem to have survived. However, all lamp lights would have been extinguished, leaving Hubert, pinned down by debris, in blackness, with subterranean chill starting to eat into his bones. Still conscious, his ears would have been straining for the sounds of a rescue party making its way to him, his only hope of survival.

Rita learned of what happened in the aftermath of the accident at her mother Betty's knee. Betty was four years old when Hubert was carried home from the mine by the willing hands of rescuers. His back was left a bloody pulp when skin was peeled away as he was pulled out of his rocky prison by his boots.

At the sight of it, Hubert's wife Elizabeth fainted so, at the height of the domestic drama, it was left to him to calmly direct Betty so she could help both her parents as best she could.

Later, as the mine was cleared of rubble, Hubert's life-saving lamp was recovered and returned to him.

Hubert, Elizabeth and Betty

Hubert was undoubtedly one of the lucky ones, as there were 120,000 deaths in British collieries between 1850 and 1972. It probably didn't feel that way when it came to returning to work and not for the first time in his life, Hubert was left with few choices. While it's likely that every sinew in his body railed against going back to the mine, he had a family to support at a time when jobs were hard to come by. Mines in Pembroke were already closing in an industry-wide slump. He was lucky, some might argue, to still keep his mining job as his own pit was profitable.

In 1934, a London-based company took over the colliery when it achieved an output of 40,000 tonnes, the highest ever recorded. Coal mining continued in the area until 1948.

But before that, Hubert had found his escape route. In the National Registration taken in 1939, his job was selling and loading timber. Later he became an insurance agent.

Afterwards, the lamp was revered by both Elizabeth and Betty, who ensured it was always gleaming. Rita's last memory of the lamp is it being lit by her grandfather and put into the engine compartment of his Austin 7 car on cold mornings to help it start.

At the Repair Shop Rita was clear about one thing – she didn't want the dents removed as they related the dramatic tale of its existence. But she did want to light it again, saying, 'We want to be sure the generations that follow on understand it has a history as a miner's lamp and also the man that used it. We must remember it saved his life.'

Initially, Steve Fletcher was left struggling to twist off the bottom in order to access the workings inside. He asked Jay to grip one end while he turned the other and between them the stubborn thread was released.

The build-up of polish, so lovingly applied down the years, was one of the reasons it couldn't be opened. It was, said Steve, a millimetre thick in places. When he had removed the old polish he applied a new layer. But it was a cautious and considered operation. He retained the vintage appearance of the metal so it didn't look like new, then he coated it with wax for a protective finish.

Inside, the wires that propelled the wick up and down were still in working order and he even recovered an original wick. Steve filled the canister, which comprised the bottom section of the lamp, with fuel. On a dark night, he left *The Repair Shop* barn and lit it to better understand the eerie glow that it would have cast in a mine. It had been an image that filled his mind as he carried out the conservation work.

When Rita returned with brother Jeff she was overwhelmed by the result of Steve's labours.

We're just so thrilled. My heart is going like a drum.

[My grandfather] was the last one to light that lamp and now we are lighting it again to remember him.

He had a tough life but he was a survivor. We are proud of that.

A VILLAGE SCHOOL'S DEEDS

I n 1839, a schoolhouse was built in a small Cambridgeshire village thanks to a parcel of land gifted by the church.

Today, it seems only right that every child should receive an education. But back then, the provision of school premises was a bold step that would enhance the lives of 'poor children' who might otherwise never have learnt to read or write. The plaque that records the School Deeds was rejuvenated at the Repair Shop and shines a light on a time when many British children better knew the pangs of hunger than any thirst for knowledge.

At the start of the nineteenth century, regular schooling was costly so it was only an elite that attended regular lessons. National schools like the one built at Barrington, which provided low-cost education for thousands more, were a church-led initiative. While the lessons might have been dry and dusty, the alternative of no education – extinguishing both prospects and potential – was worse still. It came at a time when a child was sometimes valued for all the wrong reasons, but childhood wasn't cherished at all.

Even in the early nineteenth century, it was known that universal education offered numerous benefits to society as a whole. US Founding Father Thomas Jefferson, who died in 1826, noted: 'If the children are untaught, their ignorance and vices will in future life cost us much dearer in their consequences than it would have done in their correction by a good education.' It was more succinctly put later in the century by writer Victor Hugo, who observed: 'He who opens a school, closes a prison.'

More elegantly still, twentieth-century philosopher Allan Bloom likened education to a movement from darkness to light, while journalist Sydney J. Harris insisted it turned mirrors into windows.

Unfortunately, this kind of collective wisdom was somewhat lost in industrial Britain, where burgeoning capitalism was prioritised ahead of the classroom and child labour was the norm. During the early nineteenth century, the average age that children went to work was 10 years old, although this figure fell to 8½ in cities. Youngsters at Barrington School would at last be elevated from the mire of ignorance, although enthusiasm for being at the cutting edge of education evidently wavered at times among both pupils and parents.

Those who came from farming families were frequently kept home to help pick potatoes, weed fields, keep turkeys or ferry a father's lunch to him during the harvest. Children might sew crops, act as crow-scarers, drive horses or help with haymaking themselves. In fact, with every season that rolled around, an array of different tasks presented themselves. Some children were compelled to move away from home after joining agricultural gangs, which were more formally organised, losing any opportunity for even a rudimentary education in doing so.

As late as 1883, one Barrington teacher complained: 'It seems hopeless to expect anything like satisfactory progress with the present state of attendance. Any excuse, however trivial, appears to be good enough in the opinion of parents for keeping children away.' The tribulations of teachers were reflected in rural schools everywhere with poor weather and illness also affecting school attendance.

Like today, country life also had its perils. Barrington's school records reveal a spare story about the death of a pupil in 1886 who was killed one evening when a pony he was riding bolted.

In areas like southwest Cambridgeshire, farming work pre-mechanisation was back-breaking and children ended up working all hours. Yet much about this existence might have sparked envy in their contemporaries.

There wasn't much evidence of mechanisation in mining areas like Yorkshire, Northumberland, Lancashire, Wales and Scotland, where there was a similar all-embracing work ethic for children. But here, children were dispatched underground to earn a few pennies. In the mines they had particular value, being small and able to access narrow tunnels. The tasks they undertook included unloading coal skips, sweeping, pushing wagons and hauling coal on their backs.

In 1842 – three years after the opening of Barrington School was celebrated – a report focussed on child labour in the mines stunned Victorian society. One seven-year-old told the Children's Employment Commission that he worked 12 hours a day down the pit, meaning he usually only saw daylight on Sundays. An eight-year-old girl employed as a trapper – meaning she opened and shut a ventilation door – revealed: 'It does not tire me but I have to trap without a light and I'm scared.' She worked alongside men who were naked as they toiled in the heat.

A 13-year-old from Durham, who confessed to being fearful of the mine's many hazards, admitted: 'I cannot read very well. I cannot write my name. I try to read the spelling book.'

One 17-year-old girl from Lancashire, frequently beaten by adult miners, said: 'I go to Sunday School but I cannot read or write. I go to the pit at 5 o'clock in the morning and come out at five in the evening.'

The resulting outcry led to the Mines and Collieries Act being passed that same year, which forbade women and girls of any age to work underground and introduced a minimum age of 10 for boys to work beneath the surface. It did not end the practice of sending young people into mines though.

Then there were factory children, also subjected to grotesquely long hours endured in a cacophony of noise in which they tackled fearfully dangerous jobs. Mills, where raw materials were processed, and factories, where goods were made, were by now highly mechanised. Young children – prized for being nimble and quick – worked at both long before concerns about health or safety surfaced. As 'scavengers' they were sent inside machinery to clear debris and had to make a hasty exit to avoid its moving parts. Not all made it out alive.

Although their wages were paltry, they risked a fine for numerous perceived offences, including lateness, dropping bobbins on the floors,

Barrington School in 1911

talking, going to the toilet if someone else was in there and not having washed. With working hours long and without a break, many children fell asleep at work – another punishable offence. More crucially, tiredness made them more prone to errors, which could cost them fingers, hands, arms or worse. If they were provided with a meal during the day, it was often meagre.

The scandal of child labourers moved people like Elizabeth Barrett Browning, who in response wrote a poem called 'The Cry of the Children' in 1843, four years after Barrington School was up and running.

> *For, all day, we drag our burden tiring,*
> *Through the coal-dark, underground —*
> *Or, all day, we drive the wheels of iron*
> *In the factories, round and round.*

When it's put into the context of the school at Barrington, the roll call of legislation to resolve the issues makes for sombre reading, not least for the decades it took to introduce a basic education. Children were affected by two avenues of legislation: industry and education. Industrial law-making appeared to get off on the right foot in 1802 when the Health and Morals of Apprentices Act restricted their working day to 12 hours. Many apprentices were orphans taken from workhouses and bonded to employers during their formative years. But there was little other forward thinking to be had.

In the 1819 Cotton Mills Act, the working day of 9 to 16-year-olds was limited to a dozen hours; all very laudable but nothing was done to enforce it. The next piece of stand-out legislation was the 1833 Factory Act, which banned children aged under 9 from working in factories. Those aged under 13 were restricted to a 9-hour day, with 13–18 year old limited to 12 hours, with no night working. There was also supposed to be 2 hours of schooling for children each day.

Some factories did provide teaching even before the law intervened, with Robert Owen in his mill at New Lanark being a shining example. Having bought the mill in 1799, he proceeded to install childcare and educational facilities among numerous other measures, which laid the foundations of the Co-operative movement. As early as 1810, he mooted an 8-hour day. Alas, his convictions didn't catch on.

Although in 1833 four factory inspectors were appointed to enforce the law, there was in practice little incentive for factory owners to comply.

More Factory Acts directed employers to restrict their use of child labour until, in 1891, the lower age limit for working part time in factories was set at 11 years old. From a twenty-first-century perspective, that late act – more than half a century after Barrington School opened – seems abominably belated. The fact is, every time restrictions were proposed the factory and mine owners made forceful objections, to the effect that replacing cheap child labour would make their products uncompetitive. The industrialists wanted a workforce that was biddable rather than educated, with the subtext that informed workers would demand greater rights. There was even a well-worn theory that mechanisation made the life of factory workers far easier than previously, transforming drudgery into a joy.

The prospects for children in labours away from the fields, the mines or factories were also fraught with difficulty. Girls worked at match factories without protection from the chemicals they handled and sewed clothing at home until late into the night. Children known as mudlarks scoured the banks of the River Thames in London, picking out items for sale.

Although there had been two Acts of Parliament to control the age upon which children could sweep chimneys in the middle of the nineteenth century, these were widely disregarded as once again there was no provision for enforcement. It wasn't until the publication of Charles Kingsley's novel *The Water Babies*, a fairy tale with a child sweep as its hero, that awareness was once again piqued. Finally, in 1875 – 36 years after the doors at Barrington School officially opened – the police were given powers to ensure no one under 16 was involved in chimney sweeping.

While a few parents were reluctant to have their offspring labouring for long hours doing these unsavoury tasks, the fact was, for some families, an additional wage was far more relevant than a child's education.

A cursory glance at how nineteenth-century education evolved reveals just how privileged the children at Barrington had been. Since 1811, the Church of England had been promoting the National Society for Promoting the Education of the Poor in the Principle of the Established Church in England and Wales – or National Schools. Here, religion was 'the first and chief thing taught to the poor'. Barrington was a typical example, with small school buildings put up next to churches.

That movement came in the wake of the other free school provider, this on a non-sectarian basis by what became known as the British and Foreign School Society for the Education of the Labouring and Manufacturing Classes of Society of Every Religious Persuasion – or British Schools. In these, Quaker John Lancaster pioneered the monitorial system, with numerous children in the same classroom supervised by older, more cognisant pupils. By 1851, National and British Schools combined numbered about 18,000 in Britain.

There was visceral competition between the two.

While Barrington's plaque is dated 1839, the school, in fact, opened its doors in the summer of the previous year. Rev. Michael Gibbs, whose name appears on the plaque, provided the momentum for the project, collecting cash by public subscription. When donations only amounted to £57 3s 6d, he funded the £142 shortfall himself. Although he tried to recoup his costs through a government grant, he was told the curriculum would have to be more secular before that could happen. In response, an outraged Rev. Gibbs wrote: 'I will not accept a farthing of Government money with a condition, the manifest wording of which is to undermine the continuance of a protestant established system of religious education.'

It was a huge overstatement, at a time when school inspectors were themselves Church of England clergy. But it seems the Rev. Gibbs didn't get his money back.

By 1858, the school was outgrowing the original buildings, now branded 'inadequate and inconvenient', at a time when the Church of England and the Nonconformists were still jockeying for preeminence. As the school sought more cash, a letter from Rev. Thrupp revealed that although only about 45 of the 70 families of agricultural labourers were members of the Church of England, all would send their children to the school while 'most of the dissenting labourers have their children baptised at church'. The building project was finally agreed, at a cost of less than £400.

Records show that in 1873 the cash yielded from 21 boys, 31 girls and 32 infants paying a penny per week yielded £15 15s – less than half the annual salary of the teacher or the costs of books and apparatus. While some of the shortfall was made up by the vicar, a voluntary rate on Barrington residents would be levied the following year to help cover costs.

Nationally, there were various Sunday Schools, a significant provision at the time, which often took place in neighbourhoods without a properly constituted school, as well as Ragged Schools, which began in 1818 for the destitute. Charles Dickens was inspired to write *A Christmas Carol* after visited a London Ragged School in 1843. From 1857, magistrates could send children to Industrial Schools if they were found begging, had committed petty crime or were deemed uncontrollable by their parents.

While the children of aristocrats and the middle classes did have options on education, including homeschooling, they didn't necessarily amount to much either. While Eton maintained a high reputation, headmasters like Dr John Keate, in situ there between 1809 and 1834, was renowned for flogging boys until he himself was too exhausted to continue. The shortcomings of the country's top public schools were recognised and addressed only from 1861.

Further down the social scale, Charles Dickens wrote of *Nicholas Nickleby*'s Dotheboys Hall, with its sadistic headmaster Wackford Squeers, following an anonymous tour of boarding schools in 1838, branding the institutions he saw as examples of 'the monstrous neglect of education in England'. He described Squeers and his fictitious school as 'an existing reality, purposely subdued and kept down lest they should be deemed impossible'.

Children of clerics and those sent overseas for the civil service or military found themselves at schools like this. Grammar schools began to thrive after 1840. Throughout all levels of schooling, the education of boys was prioritised over that of girls.

In 1870 the Forster Elementary Education Act broadened provision, at a time when an estimated two million children had no access to schooling, by establishing state-funded Board Schools. They were so named because they were run by elected school boards and became famous – or infamous – for teaching the so-called 3 Rs – reading, writing and arithmetic. Fees were still levied but poor parents were considered exempt.

Barrington loosened its ties to the church and became a Board School in 1879, possibly hopeful of a chance to reinvent itself. The following year, one teacher complained of 'deplorable inefficiency' saying: 'Have attempted to establish some form of discipline in the school, an item which appears to have been almost entirely ignored.'

An entry into the school log on 6 October 1883 makes for uncomfortable reading on many levels.

School closed on Monday in consequence of a most lamentable accident. One of the ... girls ... was discovered to be on fire while she was playing in the playground and before help could reach her was so badly burned that she died in two hours. In consequence, I suppose partly, of this painful occurrence the attendance fell to 58.

If there was a breakdown in discipline, it wasn't for want of effort by teachers who often resorted to physical means. A punishment book was kept to record what went on.

In 1888, one parent complained that her child had been pinched so severely by the master that her skin was marked. 'The master denied the charge but allowed that he might have punished the girl on the day in question without entering it at the end of the week in the log book … He was instructed for the future to enter punishments at the time of infliction; and to use only a suitable cane which the Treasurer was instructed to provide.'

A decade later, schooling became mandatory for five to ten-year-olds everywhere and School Attendance Officers were employed to ensure it happened, although absenteeism remained an issue. Schooling effectively became free in 1891 and the leaving age was raised to 11 two years later. The Voluntary Schools Act of 1897 helped finance Church schools. However, it wasn't until 1900 that higher elementary schools, educating 10 to 15-year-olds, were instituted, although prior to that there were workplace initiatives, including lecturers, mechanical institutes and various societies and associations that promoted further learning. Local Education Authorities were introduced by the Balfour Act in 1902 and once again, Barrington responded. That same year it became an elementary school.

By now, industrialists were minded to support a breadth of education as Britain was at risk of being overtaken as the world's industrial hub.

Records show how the school responded to the First World War. In 1915, the children sent 352 eggs to Shepreth, in south Cambridgeshire, for wound soldiers, bought with money from a house-to-house collection. The following year, nine pairs of socks were sent to soldiers at the front and ten pairs of mittens to the men aboard minesweepers.

In 1925, all children over 11 were invited to attend the senior school at Foxton, with an offer of a free bicycle and cheap dinner. Only three boys went. A full seven years later the enticement was finally scrapped.

When the Second World War broke out, place names on the school plaque were obscured with red paint, for the same reason all signposts were taken down, so they couldn't assist any invasion forces.

School numbers were boosted by evacuees, although many soon drifted back to their homes. Now the timetable included air-raid drills and gas-mask checks. According to the school records: 'The girls have completed many pairs of socks, six pairs of mittens and one pair of gloves for soldiers' use and the boys have collected iron, silver paper, paper and bones for the Women's Institute.' The children also made nightdresses for the Women's Voluntary Service and 21 blankets for the Red Cross.

With air raids in London, more evacuees came to Barrington and in 1941 there were 49 local children and 32 evacuees on the books. Former pupil Margaret recalls the arrival of two waves of evacuees at the school, making the classroom far busier than before, although the number of teachers didn't increase in consequence.

Margaret remembers school lessons being primarily English and maths classes. Her wartime recollections are more closely related to life outside the classroom – and the existence of numerous RAF stations in Cambridgeshire serving RAF fighter and bomber squadrons, as well as the United States Air Force after 1941. The closest bases to Barrington were RAF Duxford, RAF Fowlmere and RAF Bourn. Standing in her garden with her grandfather, she remembers counting the bombers taking off from a nearby airfield, then counting the number that returned. On several nights, her grandfather pointed out an ominous red glow on the horizon. 'They're getting it bad tonight,' he said. Only later did she realise it was flames from a bombing raid on London that were etched on the dark sky, some 50 miles from where she stood.

In 1969, new buildings were constructed for the infants and juniors of Barrington School. But the sign remained the same, with its daubs of red paint, and by now it was showing symptoms of its great age.

Head Gill Davies brought it into the Repair Shop for the attention of art conservator Lucia Scalisi and together they pondered what to do about the blanked-out names. For Lucia, the red paint applied more than 80 years ago had become an integral part of the object's story

The plaque displaying the school deeds

and thus should remain, but that would deny the sign any references to Barrington. Jay suggested a compromise – that one section of red paint was removed so as to reveal the village name, while the rest remained as a talking point.

Quickly, Lucia identified that the notice was painted on a sheet of metal, painted to look like wood. The panel would need careful handling. With metal being so bendy, there was a risk the original paint would flake off if it was flexed.

Lucia began with a 'spit' clean, using saliva on cotton wool to test what the surface coating might be. When nothing came off, she tried water with a drop of ammonia – this breaks the surface tension of the water, enabling it to be more effective, especially with a greasy surface coating of decades of dirt and grime.

Once the surface was cleaned, it was possible to test for the solubility of the discoloured varnish. The red paint blocking out the names of the district and school sat on top of the heavily discoloured varnish. This made cleaning complex. One saving grace though was that the red paint was water-soluble and did not dissolve in the hydrocarbon solvents used to remove the varnish. Still, it was time-consuming and the varnish was uneven in its application, with some areas thicker than others.

The cleaning process was time-consuming. The paints used were likely oil paints or general household paints readily available at the time in vermilion red, brown umber, black and an off-white background, each had a different solubility so that cleaning had to be tailored to each of the different areas.

Behind the frame was a backboard made up of what appeared to be floorboard planks. Lucia noticed not only tell-tale flight holes of woodworm, revealing that the beetle larvae had once lived there, but also evidence of frass, the powdery faeces indicating the infestation was live. Dom was on hand to remove the old wood and construct a new and more supportive plywood backing for the School Deeds.

The losses in the paint surface were too shallow to pack with a filling material, it would have just fallen out. Lucia used acrylic paint because, as well as being a sympathetic material that ages well and can easily be removed at a later date without detriment to the original paint surface, its heavy texture could fill the shallow areas of loss.

Finally, a brush-coat of synthetic resin varnish was applied to both seal the surface and to saturate the colours, making them look bright and readable.

Several spray coats of the same varnish were then applied to build up a suitable surface finish for the School Deeds.

Gill was delighted with the plaque, explaining: 'Having the sign preserved for future generations means so much as this school is the heart of the village.'

A 'RUSTY
BUCKET'

To his family, it was affectionately known as 'the rusty bucket', but to Francis Suttill the unremarkable canister he prized was an irreplaceable bond with a father he never knew.

The 'bucket' had been parachuted into occupied France during the Second World War, filled with weapons that could be used against the German army by French Resistance fighters. It was Francis' father, code name Prosper, who organised the flight and oversaw a covert distribution network. After the Gestapo discovered its existence, he was arrested, tortured and finally killed. Francis was two when his father first parachuted into France and five when he died. For decades, all connections to 'Prosper' were restricted to a series of sepia photographs until he was given the bucket, a tool of the undercover agent's trade.

With help from *The Repair Shop*, the numbers stencilled on the bucket but obscured by rust gathered over 70 years would be revealed and he would at last know for certain what it had contained.

His father, also called Francis but best remembered by his code name, was part of the Special Operations Executive, which was formed in 1940 to conduct sabotage against Hitler's forces and was otherwise known as the 'Ministry of Ungentlemanly Warfare'.

Although he was schooled in Britain, Prosper had grown up in France as his Yorkshire-born father had married a French woman and managed a textile mill in the country's industrial north. It was there that he recovered from a serious bout of polio as a teenager. While one leg was left three-quarters of an inch shorter than the other, he stoutly refused to walk with a limp.

He went on to study at French and British universities before becoming a barrister. In England, he had met and married a medical student, Margaret, and together they had dreams of building their own home in Surrey. Although they succeeded, they had problems paying for it as the world economy nose-dived. At the outbreak of war, Francis – already a father of one and perhaps hoping to alleviate the family's financial problems – enlisted, joining the East Surrey Regiment.

His war records have been lost so it's difficult to pinpoint his movements. But it's clear his potential was spotted and he was recommended for a role in SOE.

According to SOE boss Maurice Buckmaster, it wasn't just his fluency in French that made him a great fit for the job. 'Prosper had the clear intellectual vision and logical perspicacity which are often found allied to Gallic features. Dark hair and clear grey eyes, combined with a classic profile, made him striking to the close observer but it was not until he spoke that one realised the full extent of his charm and balance. It was a joy to work with a man whose brain cut like a knife into the problems we put before him.'

Still, while Francis was recruited in the spring of 1942, he had to wait for six months before parachuting into France, time spent learning the dark arts of subterfuge. Before he left Britain he was skilled in setting explosives, radio operations and forgery, all vital qualifications for his task as circuit organiser.

In a letter to his wife Margaret before he left he sounded chipper.

I have a marvellous job and an excellent team under my orders and I will do all I can to make the thing a great success.

Goodbye my darling and thank you a thousand times for all the happiness you have always given me. I am the luckiest of men.

It turned out he was not as lucky as he had believed. On landing, he dislocated the knee in his polio-affected leg and found the nearby

Francis Suttill, codename Prosper

package didn't contain clothes as expected but a radio transmitter he didn't recognise. And that was just the start …Espionage operations in an occupied territory are never easy to maintain and a network established in France before his arrival had been infiltrated and destroyed. For their part, the Germans were perpetually alert to the presence of spies.

Still, his first weeks in France were successful. Prosper went on tour, posing as an agricultural agent with courier Andrée Borrel as his wife, trying to recruit helpers for a network known as *Physician* and identify secluded clearings to serve as parachute drop zones for guns, ammunition and incoming agents. Like other agents, his brief was 'to cause the maximum damage and confusion in the shortest possible time'.

Prosper soon established a loyal corps occupying a broad sweep across the north of France, with contacts in the east in the Ardennes and in the west, close to the Atlantic.

With some chutzpah, he would meet potential volunteers in a room above a jazz club in Paris frequented by German officers. Suspicions were always running high and his prickly audiences were sometimes sceptical. So he asked them to provide him with a phrase that they would then hear repeated back to them by BBC announcers at 7.30 pm the following evening. Alerted by his radio operators, announcers back in London would duly repeat the phrase, validating Prosper's credentials.

He trained people in explosives and organised convoluted distribution schemes for incoming weaponry. Some went to the Communist groups, which acted outside London's control.

Arranging parachute drops that would provide the arms to mount operations against the Germans was challenging and often frustrating. It involved making radio contact with London and co-ordinating a team to claim the items and dispose of the packaging, all the while hoping for good weather. Then it was a case of furtively listening to the BBC to hear a pre-arranged signal read in French indicating that the promised mission was going to take place. Some of the translated signals include 'there are spectacles to follow,' 'Marcel wishes Marcel a good morning,' 'the piglets will be stuffed,' and 'the dog sneezed on the curtains'.

RAF pilots were notoriously reluctant to undertake these difficult night-time missions, which involved flying low across miles of enemy-held territory and risked planes that were perpetually in short supply. Sometimes the beacons that signified the drop zones to pilots weren't lit, the agreed identification signal wasn't flashed by operatives on the ground or pilots released their consignments in the wrong place from the air. On occasion, the planes would develop faults mid-flight and turn back. Then there was the overarching threat of being detected.

The first parachute drop Prosper orchestrated was in the middle of November 1942 on an estate in Étrépagny, Normandy. The haul contained 88lb plastic explosive, 24 sten guns, 34 revolvers, 46 grenades, 15 clam mines and 50 incendiaries. These were gathered in by fast-moving helpers, picked up by lorry, hidden in a barn, transported in a honey wagon up to the River Seine then put on a barge headed for Paris.

Although it's impossible to say precisely what operations Prosper carried out on the ground, he was linked to several goods and troop train explosions, the bombing of government buildings and providing guns that carried out random assassinations of German officers on the streets of Paris.

Yet his very success brought about problems. The larger his network grew, the greater the chances of its security being compromised. He was recalled to London in May 1943, then parachuted back into France after just five days.

A progress report to the SOE Executive Committee dated shortly afterwards declared the *Physician* circuit had made 'excellent progress' in the previous two months. Although no one knows what was discussed while he was in London, it continues '[Prosper's] short visit to this country has been of immense value'. It was the last time Margaret saw her husband, by now the father of two sons.

According to Air Ministry files, *Physician* team workers took delivery of 205 containers in June. At least one aircraft was shot down.

Prosper was captured by the Germans on 24 June after he returned to his hotel, putting up a violent struggle although he was hopelessly outnumbered. He was one domino that fell in a chain reaction, beginning when one of his lieutenants was stopped at a roadblock carrying a briefcase containing radio crystals and reports of the network's operations. Although everyone was identified by codename rather than their real identities, there was an address for Prosper's wireless operator in Paris. When Germans raided that flat they found a pile of forged identity papers on the table, including one for Prosper bearing his current address. Luck had finally deserted him and he was dispatched to the SS counterintelligence base/Gestapo headquarters in Avenue Foch. At the time the Germans were convinced there were imminent plans for invasion. There's no record of Francis' interrogation but the venue was notorious for ill-treatment of prisoners.

His wireless operator was duly compelled to make contact with London under the scrutiny of German code-breakers. Although he deliberately missed out his security code, hoping to indicate he was acting under duress, he received back a mild rebuke from London, reminding him to use it next time. The Germans were then able to decode an archive of his messages to discover the identities of local agents, painstakingly building an almost complete picture of the *Physician* network and others it intersected.

Thus the catastrophe extended far beyond Prosper and his immediate circle as the Germans seized details of hundreds of civilians in the French networks. Of some 160 French recruits who were arrested and deported to concentration camps in Germany, only half returned.

Prosper himself was taken to Sachsenhausen concentration camp near Berlin, held in solitary confinement and was shot six weeks before the conflict ended, although no official camp records of the execution exist. As everybody celebrated VE Day back in Britain, his wife Margaret had no idea if he was alive or dead. A flurry of conspiracy theories connected to the incident began to circulate; that Prosper had been double-crossed, that a fellow agent was a traitor, even that the network had been sacrificed by London for some greater good. At one point it was rumoured that Prosper and some fellow SOE prisoners escaped at the end of the war.

Son Francis eventually set about investigating his father's fate and published his findings in a book called *Prosper: Major Suttill's French Resistance Network*.

The truth, he found, was less sensational. The sprawling network collapsed because one man had been careless, carrying with him documents in a briefcase that should have been hidden. During research in London and France, he learnt more about Prosper's extraordinary courage in the face of Hitler's henchmen and the nerve-jangling, knife-edge clandestine existence he knew for the months he was in France.

Years later, as Francis investigated drop zones in France, he met Jacques Bordier who, as a lad, had helped his father Jean at three parachute drops in the Loire Valley. Although the site of the drops is now occupied by a motorway service station, Bordier was able to produce the bucket from one of them, which he presented to Francis. Jean was one of those who didn't survive deportation.

A young Francis with his father

The bucket – or cell as it's properly called – was one of three dropped inside a long metal canister manufactured by the Southern Gas Company. Each of the components bore a stencilled number that identified what it once contained.

It was for Dom to decipher the painted stencil on its side that would reveal the consignment. By any standards, it was going to be a challenging operation.

His first step was to remove as much rust as he safely could using a rust remover that wouldn't harm the remaining fragments of paintwork. Armed with information including the height of the letters on the cell, Dom contacted military museums and specialist restoration teams to find out which typeface was used at the time.

A set of authentic wartime stencils proved a vital prop. Given the precise outline he now had at his disposal, Dom then offered up each letter or number one by one, looking for evidence of white paint outside its boundaries or black inside. If there was evidence of it, then the chosen letter or number was the wrong one. He'd been convinced the most difficult to read letter was an 'S'. After rejecting 90 per cent of the letters and numbers it was clear towards the end that it was a 9 and, eventually, he solved the riddle. The code carried on the cell was B9A 9155.

Dom's next task was to enhance the code, using the finest brush he could find and stippling – painting in dots rather than strokes – to fill in the missing sections.

He was careful to only put new white paint over black paint, and not over bare metal areas, where the black had chipped away. If the black had chipped away, there would be no chance of it being originally white. Small details like that helped to tie in the restoration, to make it look like it was untouched by modern hands. After every few dabs, he stepped back to gauge the overall impression. It was imperative to stop the repair well before it started to look brand new.

The final step was to apply an oil that would stabilise the newly added paint, bring lustre to the original black paint and stop the rust encroaching any further.

When Francis returned to *The Repair Shop* barn both he and Dom were uncharacteristically nervous. Francis was anticipating the strengthening of a bond with his father by discovering what had been in the cell when it was dropped. Dom was awed by Francis' expertise and was wondering if the work he'd carried out could possibly do justice to the cell and its story.

After 'the rusty bucket' was unveiled, Francis reached into his pocket for copies of type-written records of cell contents, catalogued in the Second World War. The last four digits, he explained, were sequential packing numbers, meaning this was the 9,155th dropped in operations. It was the first three that were key to identifying its load. Until now, Francis had read the B as an 8, leaving him unable to identify it in paperwork.

Thanks to the conservation work carried out by Dom, he discovered the correct code and could reveal it brought into France two sten guns with 600 rounds of ammunition and ten magazines, plus a dozen grenades, packed with sandbags to stop them exploding on impact.

Dom felt the weight of revelation, telling Francis it was an honour to be part of his father's history. For Francis, the moment was profound.

I did not miss my father for most of my life as I had never known him so there was no loss. However, when I started my research and visited Sachsenhausen, standing in the remains of the cell he had occupied for 18 months, it did hit me that there was a gap in my life which I had never really acknowledged. My further research into his life and achievements revealed a story of heroism beyond my comprehension but which made me very proud.

A SEWING
TABLE

To a working mum in the Second World War, good neighbours were cherished individuals whose time, freely given, meant that life could continue in a version of normality. As such, next-door neighbour Auntie Jackson was held in high esteem by the Butter family, not least by toddler Christine.

She spent hours at Auntie Jackson's house in Aston; listening to the radio, looking at old photographs, preparing food for tea.

At some point during the day, Christine would ask: 'Have you got any bits for me today?' Together, the couple would make their way to the rarely used front room of the house, where a bay window overlooked the front garden. Among a stash of antique furniture, there was a treasured sewing table. To an excited Christine, this was the highlight of the day.

Already about 100 years old, the sewing table had a lid that lifted to reveal numerous angled compartments, some of them with tops on, designed to store needles, thread of all hues, buttons, ribbon, pins and other paraphernalia. For now, it stored only Auntie Jackson's crochet in its inner section.

To Christine's eye, it was filled with secret partitions in which to rummage – and her small, searching fingers always turned up a prize to take home that had been hidden especially for her. The booty might be a pressed flower, an empty cotton reel, a shiny button or even a washed pebble from the garden. No matter that the item had cost nothing, it was treated with great reverence and always proudly taken home to show her mother.

Christine's father Harry, an insurance agent in peacetime, had joined up and was now a despatch rider for the Royal Air Force, working in the Far East in oppressive humidity among the unfamiliar sights and sounds of the jungle. While he was away, Christine's mum Betty had stepped into his shoes to keep the business afloat.

After Christine was born in 1942, Betty was compelled to rely on the goodwill of neighbours for childcare. Living in a terrace, she was fortunate to have former shirtmaker Alexander Francis and his wife, Phoebe, on one side, a childless couple both in their seventies who were always keen to accommodate the youngster. Often, there were home-made jam tarts waiting for Christine when she arrived. She would sit cosily in their comfortable home, spellbound by the sound of their noisy ticking clock. Outside, there was space to skip around their tidy garden when the sun came out.

But her favourite days were spent with Auntie Jackson, on the other side, where the garden beyond the outside toilet was overgrown – although it did contain a prominent gooseberry bush where for a while Christine suspected she might have been found as a baby. Although the fire in the back room was always meagre and Auntie Jackson watered down her milk to make it last longer, there were plenty of cuddles to be had and it was from there that Christine anticipated the great domestic expeditions of discovery that centred on the sewing table.

Eventually, the war came to an end and Harry duly returned; a homecoming that was treated with great caution by his daughter. When this uniformed stranger walked up the garden path, speaking as if he knew her well, she was suspicious. That night, she refused to kiss him, opting to plant her lips on his photograph instead, just as she had done every night previously. Like other children across Britain, she had to get to know a father who'd been absent for her formative years and learn to share a mother who until now had offered her almost undivided attention.

The Butters eventually moved out of Aston to a more rural setting. It wasn't that the substantial house in Ettington Road was too small, but choking smog from factories in and around Birmingham was proving a

Christine (on the left) with Auntie Jackson on VJ Day

serious health hazard for Christine, who suffered continual bouts of bronchitis. While London was notorious for its 'pea soup' fogs, there were similar problems in all industrialised areas. Before they moved, Christine has memories of her mother walking in front of the family car swinging a torch, so her father could slowly but safely wend his way to an appointment. The first Clean Air Act came in 1956 to help eradicate the menace.

Although they moved from the area, the Butters continued to visit and in adulthood, Christine remained in touch with her by now ageing babysitter. For her part, Auntie Jackson obviously held those memories made during the war years as closely as Christine did herself. When the older woman died in 1971 aged 83, she left an astonished and delighted Christine the sewing table.

It was nearly 50 years after that when Christine brought it to the Repair Shop, with the sewing table by now appearing very much past its prime. Water damage to the lid had lifted a section of veneer, the lock was broken and carving on the central support was chipped. For wood restorer Will, there was plenty to keep him busy.

Auntie Jackson's real name was Helen and she was a spinster who'd spent her working life as a clerk. Christine occasionally played with Helen's niece Heather, who was a similar age.

Like Christine, Helen had been born in Aston, but at the time it was separated from Birmingham on the political landscape. These neighbouring industrial heartlands were amalgamated in 1911 by local authority boundary changes. Although her father Charles was a schoolmaster and her neighbours in Rifle Crescent included a professor of music and people of private means, most of the terraced housing was occupied by industrial workers and included a silversmith, goldsmith, brass tube maker and lathe operator. There was a railway clerk, signalman, engine cleaner and stoker as well as tailors, accounts clerks, a rent collector and some shop assistants.

While Helen – known to her family as Nell – soon got a job at a timber merchants, mother Sarah, born in 1860, stayed at home and it was perhaps she who made best use of the sewing table. Sarah lived through a time when the middle class was growing in number and the women in it were judged on the quality of their needlecraft. Sewing tables, which began appearing in the last part of the eighteenth century, provided not only ample storage but a smooth, clean surface on which to stitch. A well-stocked sewing table became an essential symbol of domestic success.

While the sewing table has linked two families across the generations, sewing itself has connected women, for better and for worse, through decades, especially in the last two centuries.

Wealthier women might have decorative cut steel or silver sewing tools stored in their table, or monogrammed thimbles. Embroidery was an expression of art and fashion but also femininity, prudence and virtue. It was an embodiment of the traditional role of women in the home. While they weren't legally permitted to have property of their own until a law change in 1870, the sewing table was a woman's unchallenged domain. It was among the few items she could bequeath to daughters or friends when she died.

Florence Nightingale was among the women who rebelled against middle-class sewing culture and all it represented, refusing to wed on the grounds that marriage would shackle her to household duties when she wanted to make her mark on the world of nursing instead. Her fear was that she was expected to be 'singing Schubert, reading the Review [or] busy embroidering, sitting around a table in the drawing-room, looking at prints, doing worsted work and reading little books'.

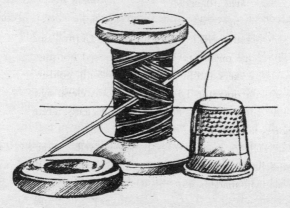

Charlotte Brontë, Elizabeth Gaskell and Elizabeth Barrett Browning all used sewing as a metaphor to underscore a frustration in middle-class women's existences.

Of course, sewing wasn't entirely the preserve of women. Tailors were traditionally male, while servicemen were always responsible for mending their own clothes. Nor was it purely a feature of the hallowed world belonging to ladies of leisure.

Some women also sewed because they had to earn a living, no matter that being a shirt, dress or hat maker usually meant low pay and appalling conditions, especially in winter months when natural light was at a premium. The struggle to sew by candle or gaslight put a colossal strain on eyesight, and the bent posture adopted by a seamstress as she leaned in towards the light induced a painful curvature of the spine. As the foundation of the industry was piecework, women and even children needed to work all hours even to eat.

In February 1841, the Children's Employment Commission heard harrowing evidence about the dressmaking business of the era, when it was often known as 'slop-work'.

The common hours of business are from 8 am till 11 pm in the winters; in the summer from 6 or half-past 6 am till 12 at night. During the fashionable season, that is from April till the latter end of July, it frequently happens that the ordinary hours are greatly exceeded; if there is a drawing-room or grand fete, or mourning to be made, it often happens that the work goes on for 20 hours out of the 24, occasionally all night.

The general result of the long hours and sedentary occupation is to impair seriously and very frequently to destroy the health of the young women. The digestion especially suffers, and also the lungs: pain to the side is very common, and the hands and feet die away from want of circulation and exercise, 'never seeing the outside of the door from Sunday to Sunday.' [One cause] is the short time which is allowed by ladies to have their dresses made.

As a result, the seamstress became a focus of concern for social reformers, often featuring in literature as downtrodden and desperate. The plight of workers like these was the subject of a Thomas Hood poem in 1843, called 'The Song of the Shirt', which started with this verse:

> *With fingers weary and worn*
> *With eyelids heavy and red*
> *A woman sat in unwomanly rags*
> *Plying her needle and thread*
> *Stich! Stitch! Stitch!*
> *In poverty, hunger and dirt*
> *And still with a voice of dolorous pitch*
> *She sang the 'Song of the Shirt'.*

Yet times were about to change – although not necessarily for the better – with the advent of the sewing machine. Although it wasn't the first, the most ubiquitous was manufactured by Isaac Singer from 1851 in the US. Some were set into a table and operated by a treadle, while others were more portable – although heavy – and sat on a table, to be powered by the turn of a handle.

For the creative upper and middle classes who first had access to sewing machines, there was now an opportunity to make fashionable clothes of choice, rather than wait for shops wedded to traditional styles to change tack. With the arrival of bicycles, for example, women could make specially designed costumes that were called skirts but were really trousers. Women could also run up banners for the suffragette movement campaigning for votes for women, which was starting make itself heard at the end of the nineteenth century.

At this time the sewing machine was a signal of status for women, but when prices dropped it became more utilitarian and began to beckon in the era of factory-made clothing, with women working faster than ever before.

Sweat shops still existed, notoriously in London's East End, and remained a concern. A House of Lords Select Committee report in

1890 told of women who worked in appalling circumstances for low pay. Labouring from 7 in the morning until 11 at night, women shirtmakers had the hire of the sewing machine, the costs of the oil needed to keep it running smoothly and even the thread deducted from their paltry wages. Many fell into arrears with the Singer Manufacturing Company but faced destitution if the machine was taken away.

For many years, those who sewed for a living were associated with prostitution. Indeed, many women did have to supplement their small incomes. But the association with prostitution was probably made because there were few options for jobs at a time when many women were family breadwinners. These became desperate and angry women.

It's presumably why one famous Suffragette chose to impersonate just such a worker in Edwardian times. Furious that working-class suffragettes were being treated so badly in prison, campaigning aristocrat Constance Lytton disguised herself as Jane Wharton, 'an ugly London seamstress'. In 1910 during a two-week spell of imprisonment, she was force-fed eight times and slapped around the face by a doctor.

Department stores began to offer a step up for dressmakers. However, that usually only followed a two-year apprenticeship, which paid nothing at all.

Wearing white overalls and working at cloth-covered tables, the dressmakers worked on quality outfits, while machinists fitted garment linings.

Clothes manufacturing took a back seat during the Second World War when the government message of 'make do and mend' was embraced in British households now limited by clothes rationing. Women dusted off their mothers' machines to make their own clothes and those of their children, using worn bedding for everyday garments and parachute silk if it was available for 'best'.

But after the war, the demand for factory-made clothes was unfettered in fashion-conscious western societies. High-profile problems of sweat-shop labour at home and abroad have occasionally dominated headlines as a taste for fast fashion that's worn once then discarded has brought misery to the lives of seamstresses. With some prescience, Thomas Hood addressed this core issue in another verse:

O, men, with sisters dear
O, men, with mothers and wives
It is not linen you're wearing out
But human creatures' lives!
Stitch! Stitch! Stitch!
In poverty, hunger and dirt
Sewing at once, with a double thread
A Shroud as well as a Shirt.

Christine was captivated with the table from childhood and interestingly she was, in fact, the latest in a family line that had survived and thrived through sewing. Her great uncle was a tailor, who typically sat cross-legged on a table while he worked, so the clothes he was sewing didn't come into contact with the dusty floor.

Her grandmother Jesse was also a tailor, who in turn taught her children Harry, Marjorie and Thora the necessary skills. Harry and his two sisters would sit up late into the night, helping her finish customers' clothes. One sister stitched the buttonholes, while the other did the hem. Harry would work the treadle machine, finishing longer seams.

Much later, Harry made clothes for his wife and sewed a feather-filled sleeping bag from parachute silk for Betty and Christine to use in the air-raid shelter in their back garden, to protect against the biting cold when the Luftwaffe targeted the industrial heartlands.

In time, he taught Christine to sew and in turn she made clothes for her three children. Now she is thrilled that one of her granddaughters is going to celebrate the family heritage by studying historical costume design. It is to her the sewing table will one day be bequeathed.

While Christine saw the table with its cracked top as a dull shadow of its former self, Will saw potential. Certainly, the walnut veneer was fragile and flaky. For some, there would be a temptation to rip off the remainder and replace with a single new sheet. However, Will wanted to retain the original character of the table as Christine would have remembered it, which meant repairing rather than removing the damaged veneer. His first step was to consolidate it by fixing the loose pieces back into place. Using glue and a veneer hammer, he attached the flapping pieces, then clamped a cling-film covered block on to the lid to hold the repair securely in place until it bonded.

The central part that needed patching was now revealed. Before choosing the right replacement piece, Will needed to clean up the rest of the lid so its true colour was exposed. It's the kind of job for which methylated spirits is a stock choice, but to use it would have been to risk the ethanol seeping into nooks and crannies and softening the glue. Given the relative thickness of the veneer, he instead chose fine sandpaper attached to an electric sander to reveal the grain. Will then applied a thin layer of polish to reveal the lustre of the walnut and picked a replacement piece that bore similar swirling patterns. He made a template of the missing pieces and tentatively cut them out in several sections, checking that they jigsawed together. The new shapes now needed to be set into the surface, with Will opting for a glue. Although he could have used wood glue, he went for a more traditional choice.

After the glueing and clamping process was repeated, the sewing-table top was once again flat and smooth. It was now time to disguise the fracture marks created by the repair using shellac. Will built up thin layers with the help of polish, pigments and stains. It was time-consuming work but loading up too much at a time risked the wood looking artificially enhanced.

While the tabletop was drying, he turned to its central support where a section of carved wood in a decorative collar was missing. His first step was to add in a piece of the appropriate size to mirror the outline. Will chose mahogany, which was much lighter than the table but it's far easier to stain a light wood than to reduce the colour of a dark piece. Once it was firmly in place, it served as a blank canvas for his carving, where he aimed to reproduce the same pattern appearing on other sections. Using a fine-liner pen, he marked the intricacies of the design and slowly made a start. Carving out too much would have entailed attaching more wood, so it was slow, considered work.

Using wax to achieve a final lustre, the table was returned to Christine. When the covering blanket was drawn away, she was transported back in time.

As she ran her fingertips across the smooth and flawless table surface, mimicking her actions of 75 years previously, she confirmed how well-loved and used objects have an ability to transcend time: 'The years have just fallen away, it is as if I'm a child again.'

A LIFEBOAT
BINNACLE

F or three teenagers, it was an adventure to rival anything in the *Boy's Own Papers* they read when they were younger. The trio had been forced off a merchant ship crossing the Atlantic by a U-boat crew and cast adrift on the waves to await rescue.

Clinging to the sides of a lifeboat as it bobbed about on the ocean, they then witnessed a dramatic ducking-and-diving battle between aircraft and submarine, with two of the planes ditching into the sea. Hours later, they clambered aboard destroyer HMS *Tartar*, none the worse for the escapade.

When it became clear that there was no room aboard the warship for the two lifeboats that had saved them, their father thought quickly. Hoping for a memento of the extraordinary incident, he identified the lifeboat binnacle, which was about to be lost forever. Happily, he was allowed to wrench it off, providing the family with a precious keepsake attached to a lively anecdote that has thrilled future generations.

Inevitably, the binnacle suffered from the ravages of increasing age and a house move. Silversmith Brenton West was the adept *Repair Shop* expert who could turn back time on the instrument.

A binnacle is a case that holds nautical instruments, particularly the magnetic compass. It's designed to keep the compass level as a vessel pitches and rolls in open sea and is usually found near the helm. Although it had suffered dents and a glass covering was missing, at least this binnacle had been saved from becoming more barnacle-covered debris on an ocean floor that was becoming a graveyard. For while the boys involved were thrilled to be part of a maritime great escape, they had no idea how close a call it had been.

The date was Thursday, 14 September 1939 and the Halnan family were travelling from Montreal, Canada, back to Britain on the SS *Fanad Head*, a 22-year-old steam-powered boat, whose principal purpose for the crossing was to transport general cargo and grain.

The boys' father, Edward Halnan, was an academic and an authority on feeding farm animals. He'd been on a lecture tour of North America with wife Adelaide and twins Keith and Geoffrey, aged 19, with 14-year-old Patrick joining him for a holiday at its end.

Britain had declared war just 11 days previously, yet still the trip didn't seem like an unnecessary risk. The focus of the fighting for the time being was in Poland, where the national army was trying to fend off German advances. The Halnans were veteran travellers and while everyone knew there were U-boats roaming the routes that the merchant ship would be taking, international protocol dictated that passengers and crew would remain unharmed. And that's largely what occurred.

Fanad Head was hunted down by U-30, under the captaincy of Fritz-Julius Lemp, who fired a shot across her bow to bring her to a halt. The stand-off occurred about 280 miles off the Irish coast. Following Lemp's instructions, the crew of 33, their Captain George Pinkerton and 8 fare-paying passengers, including the Halnans, donned their bulky Mae West life jackets and climbed into two lifeboats, with crewmen manning the oars. The U-boat even gave one of the lifeboats a tow to help get it out of the danger zone. But unbeknown to the Germans, an SOS had been dispatched from the British ship before it was abandoned.

Although some 200 miles distant, HMS *Ark Royal* picked up the signal and launched three Blackburn Skua aircraft in their direction. It would be the first action the Royal Navy's Fleet Air Arm saw in the conflict.

As the planes were arrowing through the sky to reach the *Fanad Head*, a five-strong German 'prize crew' was climbing aboard to plunder provisions before scuttling it.

When a first low-flying Skua arrived, the pilot was surprised to see the U-boat on the surface alongside the ship. In a rush to action, he

The lifeboat being prepared for launch

dropped bombs that exploded before they reached the surface of the sea. The blast damaged the tail of the plane, which plunged into the waves. Both crewmen escaped, although they were badly burnt and only one made it to the *Fanad Head*. When he reached the ship, R. J. Thurstan was pulled out of the water unconscious. The observer, Petty Officer James Simpson, 35, a married man from Gosport, was never found.

At the sight of the plane, the U-boat had crash dived, even though one man was marooned on its outside deck. He also now swam to the ship, to be hoisted up to safety by two fellow crew members. The other three had sustained injuries in the brief attack.

Ten minutes later, a second Skua arrived, dropping a 100lb bomb on what the crew perceived to be a submarine. They reported seeing two men swimming in the water. In retrospect, it seems likely they targeted the sinking Skua as U-30 emerged out of the water during the melee, only to be forced down again by a volley of machine-gun fire from the plane. Low on fuel, the second plane turned around to head back for the *Ark Royal*.

Uncertainly, the U-boat surfaced once more to retrieve their missing crew members – just as a third Skua hovered into view, flying at a low level and keen to unleash its firepower. For a second time, the force of the bomb disabled the plane rather than the intended target and the Skua was lost to the waves. This time, the observer didn't make it out in time and 24-year-old George McKay, who was married and from Kent, perished in the plane. Pilot Lt Guy 'Griff' Griffiths swam to the ship, to join his pilot colleague and six Germans. (Almost certainly, the planes were lost because of a fault in the way the fuses on the bombs were rigged.)

Initially, both pilots refused to board the submarine, until Lemp told them it was about to be torpedoed. Abruptly changing their minds, they were duly taken prisoner just as a flight of Swordfish aircraft appeared, strafing U-30 as it slid beneath the waves and finally out of sight of the watching Halnans.

The Swordfish flew past the lifeboats, signalling that help was on its way. It's just one of the shots Geoffrey Halnan captured with the camera that he had rescued from his belongings before leaving his cabin. Much

The crew and passengers cheering the
Swordfish as it flies overhead

later, he and his family watched in relief and some degree of awe as HMS *Tartar* sailed close to the lifeboats so those aboard could climb the rope ladder fixed to its side. Adelaide lost a shoe as she did so.

Five days later, U-30 appeared in Reykjavik harbour, Iceland, where injured crewmember Adolf Schmidt was put ashore for treatment. He was duly taken prisoner when the British invaded Iceland in May 1940. Pilots Thurstan and Griffiths were then landed at Wilhelmshaven and, after initially being regarded as political prisoners, were finally taken to a prisoner-of-war camp in Brunswick.

But what no one knew that day is that Lemp had a terrible secret, which only emerged after that lengthy patrol was completed. Against all accepted rules of warfare, it had been on his orders that the SS *Athenia* was sunk the day that war had been declared, with the loss of more than 100 lives. He'd not only gone against the international norms of warfare but acted against the express order of his Führer.

How had this colossal error of judgement occurred? Studying the target through his periscope, Lemp saw what he thought was a darkened armed merchant vessel zig-zagging through the water as if to avoid submarine engagement, just as a military vessel might. In fact, the SS *Athenia* was a liner bound for Canada with a large number of American passengers and evacuee children aboard.

Despite the mutual declarations of war, Hitler was still confident of striking a deal with Britain – and in any event, he was keen to keep the United States at arms-length from the conflict. He had told his fleet of U-boats to follow what was known as Prize Regulations, which prohibited unannounced attacks on passenger ships. Under those rules, merchant ships could be stopped, searched and even sunk, as long as the occupants were made safe.

Lemp made a terrible mistake, probably with the recently received coded message of the submarine fleet commander Karl Donitz at the forefront of his mind: 'Hostilities with England effective immediately.' He assessed the target one final time before preparing to fire the first torpedoes in the Battle of the Atlantic. After they had ripped through the water and made contact with *Athenia*, he turned his vessel away rather than assist people trying to escape the holed ship. As it happened, the weather was kind and the ship did not sink immediately, giving rescue vessels time to reach the scene. Still, the death toll sounded shocking when Donitz heard the news of the sinking on the BBC.

Hitler's propaganda chief Joseph Goebbels responded with a rearguard action, claiming there were no U-boats in the vicinity at the time, even blaming the loss on Britain. Yet when Lemp finally got to Wilhelmshaven, it seemed like everyone in the U-boat command knew what had happened. However, Donitz chose not to remonstrate with his young captain, a superb operator who had returned victorious from his first patrol having claimed the *Athenia* and the *Fanad Head*. Fortunately, for reasons unknown, Lemp decided to follow orders on the day he encountered the Halnans on the *Fanad Head*.

It wasn't until 1946 that the truth about the events that day was revealed. By then, Lemp was dead, bizarrely – and without meaning to – having helped Britain win the war. In May 1941, Lemp had moved on to U-110 and was attacking a British convoy south of Iceland when the craft was disabled by a depth charge. The submarine was abandoned by its crew who thought it was doomed. However, a boarding party from HMS *Bulldog* had time to scavenge an Enigma machine and its cipher books.

There are two differing stories about Lemp's fate. Some German survivors insist he was shot in the back by the British. However, another version has him swimming back to his vessel to destroy the top-secret kit aboard and drowning in the process. Either way, his final thoughts would

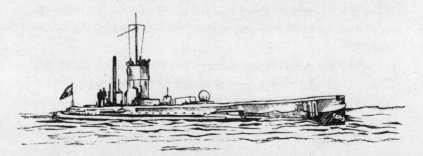

have been how the loss of Germany's technological prowess would likely skewer Hitler's ambition. In great secrecy, the Enigma machine was taken to Bletchley Park and used by Alan Turing to crack the necessary codes that governed the complex system. After that was achieved, the Battle of the Atlantic was won.

Back on HMS *Tartar*, the Halnans were presented with a grim reality check of how close a call they'd had. As it made its way up to Scotland where the family would be landed, the destroyer ploughed through jetsam from SS *Athenia* in a broad field that spoke of terrible destruction.

The business of war got more serious still for the family, with Patrick and Keith both serving in Burma, while Geoffrey taught RAF pilots and ground crews the principles of the innovative application of radar. All of them survived and went on to Cambridge University, where both parents had been students. (However, Cambridge University did not recognise women graduates at the time, with the first degree for a woman being given in 1948 to Queen Elizabeth, wife of George VI and the present queen's mother.)

Patrick entered the legal profession and eventually became a High Court judge. Keith trained as a doctor and finished his career as an eminent cancer specialist, while Geoffrey worked as a top-flight naval scientist. They all had children – who have all since had families of their own. The binnacle evolved as a life-affirming object for a family that might never have been.

Geoffrey's daughter Jo, who brought the binnacle into the Repair Shop, said: 'If my family hadn't been rescued I wouldn't be here today.' It was also a poignant reminder of her father, who relished telling the story of his family's early encounter with the enemy during the Second World War.

When the story of the binnacle unfolded, Brenton caught his breath. The ship it came from was named for a peninsula in Donegal, Ireland, where for generations his wife's family had been regular visitors. A family home there stood above a lonely beach and had panoramic views of the sea. It remains one of the most isolated and spectacular points on the coast.

Given its history, it was no surprise that the binnacle was somewhat battered by the time its constituent parts reached the Repair Shop. The compass was detachable but some parts of the container were missing altogether. Brenton's first impression of the brass case is that he had a long task of smoothing out numerous dents in its metalwork.

It seemed someone had already tried a renovation project on the binnacle, possibly adding more bumps and dips in the process. Using the flat side of a file, Brenton rubbed the surface to identify where they all were. Surface dirt was ground away from the lumps by the file, leaving the high marks shiny, while low spots out of the reach of the blade retained a dull appearance. Then he put the binnacle on a steel stake and gently worked away with a hammer to smooth the exterior. It was hours of painstaking work.

Only when the brass was in better shape did he set about fixing the structural damage around its seams. Brenton is no stranger to soldering, but on this occasion, he was mindful that if the flame was too hot it might fatally weaken the joints in the metal. The key was to achieve just enough heat to melt the solder so it could flow into position but no more. When it came to a larger gap, he turned the binnacle on its side so gravity could play its part in channelling the solder where it needed to go. Thanks to his experience, the repairs were robust and came at no risk to the casing.

When it came to polishing the brass, Brenton had the advantage of a mechanised disc that would have achieved a gleam of newness. But he'd been careful not remove every last dent, so it had a fitting appearance for an object of its age.

For a while, the hole in its side was something of a mystery until internet research revealed it's where a compartment for a lamp would have been attached so that those condemned to a lifeboat on the ocean at night could still tell in which direction they were headed. It was down to Brenton to reproduce one and he started by making a paper template.

With brass sheet ordered in by Jay, he cut out shapes that corresponded to the pattern using a saw. One section was going to be the bottom of the compartment, the other formed three sides, with the fourth being the binnacle itself. Joining the metalwork called for narrow seams and 90-degree angles, so Dom rolled a heavyweight folding machine into the workshop to assist. By carefully lining up the metal, they could make a right angle and leave a width of just a few millimetres to slide into the framework on the side of the binnacle. Soon a box-like shape came together with a hinged-access door replacing the one that had been lost years before.

The binnacle's wooden stand – which was probably a later addition – had been sent to Will's work station. Not only was it wobbly, it looked tired and worn. His first task was to remove a cork ring on the bottom. He determined to replace the cork with green baize to give it a more even keel. Then he used sandpaper to remove all traces of surface dirt and wax before applying an English walnut stain, adding a richness to the wood bleached out years ago by salty air and sea spray. The result was so successful Will was concerned about outshining Brenton's handiwork. As for Brenton, he couldn't believe the same piece of wood was being returned.

While the binnacle was at the Repair Shop, Jo had been reflecting on all it meant to her. 'It isn't just an item, it's the story that goes with it,' she explained. 'I've been thinking about how vulnerable they were in that lifeboat and the U-boat torpedoing their ship. The compass represents all that. It is going to take pride of place in my lounge so that when I have visitors I'm going to relate the story just as my father used to enjoy doing.'